Socket.IO Cookbook

Over 40 recipes to help you create real-time JavaScript applications using the robust Socket.IO framework

Tyson Cadenhead

BIRMINGHAM - MUMBAI

Socket.IO Cookbook

First published: October 2015

Production reference: 1081015

Published by Packt Publishing Ltd.
Livery Place
35 Livery Street
Birmingham B3 2PB, UK.

ISBN 978-1-78588-086-5

www.packtpub.com

Credits

Author
Tyson Cadenhead

Reviewers
Gonzalo Ayuso
George Brassey

Commissioning Editor
Amarabha Banerjee

Acquisition Editor
Reshma Raman

Content Development Editor
Mayur Pawanikar

Technical Editor
Siddhesh Ghadi

Copy Editor
Relin Hedly

Project Coordinator
Kranti Berde

Proofreader
Safis Editing

Indexer
Mariammal Chettiyar

Graphics
Disha Haria

Production Coordinator
Conidon Miranda

Cover Work
Conidon Miranda

About the Author

Tyson Cadenhead works as a senior JavaScript engineer at Aloompa in Nashville, Tennessee. He has dedicated his professional career to building large-scale applications in JavaScript and Node. Tyson addresses audiences at various conferences and programming meetups on how to build real-time web applications with Socket.IO or Meteor.js. He blogs on topics such as JavaScript and web technologies at `http://www.tysoncadenhead.com`.

Tyson lives in the greater Nashville area with his wife and two sons, where he enjoys gardening, raising chickens, reading philosophy and economics books, and playing guitar.

About the Reviewers

Gonzalo Ayuso is a web architect and specializes in open source technologies. He has more than 15 years of experience in web development. Gonzalo holds extensive experience in delivering scalable, secure, and high-performance web solutions to large-scale enterprise clients.

He has a varied background, especially in providing backend code. Gonzalo mainly focuses on Internet technologies, databases, mobile development, and programming languages, especially PHP, Python, and JavaScript. He blogs at `http://gonzalo123.com`. Gonzalo also likes to speak at technology conferences and organize coding dojos. You can also follow him on Twitter at `@gonzalo123`.

George Brassey is a developer from London. He loves art, music, and technology. George earned a degree in cinema studies from the New York University and worked in the film industry before switching to software development. He enjoys projects where technology intersects with the arts. George currently works with an expert team at Paddle8, building the future of online art auctions.

www.PacktPub.com

Support files, eBooks, discount offers, and more

For support files and downloads related to your book, please visit www.PacktPub.com.

Did you know that Packt offers eBook versions of every book published, with PDF and ePub files available? You can upgrade to the eBook version at www.PacktPub.com and as a print book customer, you are entitled to a discount on the eBook copy. Get in touch with us at service@packtpub.com for more details.

At www.PacktPub.com, you can also read a collection of free technical articles, sign up for a range of free newsletters and receive exclusive discounts and offers on Packt books and eBooks.

https://www2.packtpub.com/books/subscription/packtlib

Do you need instant solutions to your IT questions? PacktLib is Packt's online digital book library. Here, you can search, access, and read Packt's entire library of books.

Why Subscribe?

- Fully searchable across every book published by Packt
- Copy and paste, print, and bookmark content
- On demand and accessible via a web browser

Free Access for Packt account holders

If you have an account with Packt at www.PacktPub.com, you can use this to access PacktLib today and view 9 entirely free books. Simply use your login credentials for immediate access.

Table of Contents

Preface

Socket.IO is an excellent library for real-time messaging between the client side and the server side. Whether you want to create a chat room in your browser, reload your hybrid mobile application, or push fresh data to an internal dashboard, this book will show you how to do it.

What this book covers

Chapter 1, Wiring It Up, provides a quick introduction to Socket.IO. It tells you how to get up and running with a Node server. This chapter concludes with debugging tips for the server and the client.

Chapter 2, Creating Real-Time Dashboards, talks about how to stream data from the server to the client. It covers how to emit MongoDB data and how to handle Socket.IO connection timeouts.

Chapter 3, Having Two-Way Conversations, provides several recipes on how to build a two-way communication. From the quintessential chat room example to a fun recipe on how to create a real-time tic-tac-toe game, it includes several other topics.

Chapter 4, Building a Room with a View, explores views and namespaces and how they can be used to target your events to specific consumers.

Chapter 5, Securing Your Data, takes a look at how to secure the Socket.IO communication with various forms of authentication, including how to lock down the HTTP referrer and how to use secure web sockets.

Chapter 6, Performing a Load Balancing Act, covers various techniques for load-balancing Socket.IO, focusing on technologies such as Redis, Memcached, and RabbitMQ.

Chapter 7, Streaming Binary Data, explores topics ranging from emitting images as data to streaming video and audio.

Chapter 8, Integrating With Mobile Applications, talks about various techniques for using Socket.IO in mobile applications. It also provides a recipe for how to trigger hot deploys from Socket.IO.

What you need for this book

This book was written using a Macbook Air running Node. However, Node and Socket.IO can be run on a Windows or Linux machine as well.

All the software used in this book is free and open source. You will definitely need to be running Node for most of the recipes. There are also some sections that cover MongoDB, Redis, Memcached, and RabbitMQ.

Who this book is for

If you have some knowledge of JavaScript and Node.js and want to create awe-inspiring application experiences with real-time communication, then this book is for you. Developers with knowledge of other languages should also be able to easily follow along.

Sections

In this book, you will find several headings that appear frequently (Getting ready, How to do it…, How it works…, There's more…, and See also).

To give clear instructions on how to complete a recipe, we use these sections as follows:

Getting ready

This section tells you what to expect in the recipe and describes how to set up any software or any preliminary settings required for the recipe.

How to do it…

This section contains the steps required to follow the recipe.

How it works…

This section usually consists of a detailed explanation of what happened in the previous section.

There's more...

This section consists of additional information about the recipe in order to make the reader more knowledgeable about the recipe.

See also

This section provides helpful links to other useful information for the recipe.

Conventions

In this book, you will find a number of text styles that distinguish between different kinds of information. Here are some examples of these styles and an explanation of their meaning.

Code words in text, folder names, filenames, file extensions, pathnames, dummy URLs, and user input are shown as follows: "We can include Socket.IO by using the `require('socket.io')` statement."

A block of code is set as follows:

```
var io = require('socket.io');

io.on('connection', function (socket) {
     socket.emit('connected');
});
```

New terms and important words are shown in bold. Words that you see on the screen, for example, in menus or dialog boxes, appear in the text like this: "For this example we will use Redis to propagate our state across servers."

Warnings or important notes appear in a box like this.

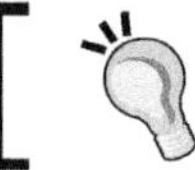

Tips and tricks appear like this.

Reader feedback

Feedback from our readers is always welcome. Let us know what you think about this book—what you liked or disliked. Reader feedback is important for us as it helps us develop titles that you will really get the most out of.

To send us general feedback, simply e-mail `feedback@packtpub.com`, and mention the book's title in the subject of your message.

If there is a topic that you have expertise in and you are interested in either writing or contributing to a book, see our author guide at `www.packtpub.com/authors`.

Customer support

Now that you are the proud owner of a Packt book, we have a number of things to help you to get the most from your purchase.

Downloading the example code

You can download the example code files from your account at `http://www.packtpub.com` for all the Packt Publishing books you have purchased. If you purchased this book elsewhere, you can visit `http://www.packtpub.com/support` and register to have the files e-mailed directly to you.

Downloading the color images of this book

We also provide you with a PDF file that has color images of the screenshots/diagrams used in this book. The color images will help you better understand the changes in the output. You can download this file from: `https://www.packtpub.com/sites/default/files/downloads/08650S_ColorImages.pdf`.

Errata

Although we have taken every care to ensure the accuracy of our content, mistakes do happen. If you find a mistake in one of our books—maybe a mistake in the text or the code—we would be grateful if you could report this to us. By doing so, you can save other readers from frustration and help us improve subsequent versions of this book. If you find any errata, please report them by visiting `http://www.packtpub.com/submit-errata`, selecting your book, clicking on the Errata Submission Form link, and entering the details of your errata. Once your errata are verified, your submission will be accepted and the errata will be uploaded to our website or added to any list of existing errata under the Errata section of that title.

To view the previously submitted errata, go to `https://www.packtpub.com/books/content/support` and enter the name of the book in the search field. The required information will appear under the Errata section.

Piracy

Piracy of copyrighted material on the Internet is an ongoing problem across all media. At Packt, we take the protection of our copyright and licenses very seriously. If you come across any illegal copies of our works in any form on the Internet, please provide us with the location address or website name immediately so that we can pursue a remedy.

Please contact us at `copyright@packtpub.com` with a link to the suspected pirated material.

We appreciate your help in protecting our authors and our ability to bring you valuable content.

Questions

If you have a problem with any aspect of this book, you can contact us at `questions@packtpub.com`, and we will do our best to address the problem.

1
Wiring It Up

In this chapter, we will cover the following recipes:

- Creating a Node HTTP server with Socket.IO
- Creating an Express server with Socket.IO
- Using Socket.IO as a cross-browser WebSocket
- Debugging on the client
- Debugging on the server

Introduction

Socket.IO is a powerful tool for creating real-time applications with bidirectional communication between the server side and the client side. It leverages the power of WebSockets along with several fallbacks, including JSON long polling and JSONP long polling through a single unified API. It can be used to create bidirectional interactions, such as real-time dashboards, chat applications, and multiplayer games.

In my previous jobs, I created several real-time JavaScript dashboards predating the Socket.IO library. During that time, I felt the pain of not having a good solution for true real-time communication. I found myself using hacks to obtain new data from the user interface. One method was to pound the server with an Ajax call every few seconds. The server had no way of knowing whether anything had updated since the last request, so it would dump all the data into the huge JSON object. It was up to the client-side JavaScript application to search the data and check whether there were any updates. If there were updates, the client side was responsible for updating the display as needed. This turned out to be difficult to maintain and a nightmare to debug. When Socket.IO was released, I was blown away. Now, I could send only the pieces of data that had actually been updated from the server instead of pushing up everything. Instead of setting an interval to make Ajax calls, I could just send data when new data came in. In short, Socket.IO made my life easier.

Socket.IO is an open source library created by Guillermo Rauch. It is built with Engine.IO, which is a lower-level abstraction on top of the WebSocket technology. Socket.IO is used to communicate bidirectionally between the server side and the client side in a syntax that looks as if you are just triggering and listening to events. The WebSocket API protocol was standardized in 2011. It is a **Transmission Control Protocol** (**TCP**) that only relies on HTTP for its initial handshake. After the handshake is complete, the connection is left open so that the server and the client can pass messages back and forth as needed.

For reference, a typical WebSocket connection without Socket.IO will look something similar to the following code on the client side:

We are not falling back for browsers that do not support WebSockets.

```
if ('Websocket' in window) {
    var ws = new WebSocket('ws://localhost:5000/channel');

    ws.onopen = function () {
        ws.send('Hello world');
    };

    ws.onmessage = function (e) {
        console.log(e.data);
    };

    ws.onclose = function () {
        console.warn('WebSocket disconnected');
    }

} else {
    throw new Error('This browser does not support websockets');
}
```

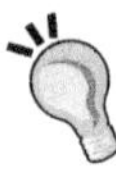

Downloading the example code

You can download the example code files from your account at `http://www.packtpub.com` for all the Packt Publishing books you have purchased. If you purchased this book elsewhere, you can visit `http://www.packtpub.com/support` and register to have the files e-mailed directly to you.

Socket.IO goes a step beyond just providing an easy-to-use and more robust API on top of WebSockets. It also provides the ability to seamlessly use other real-time protocols if WebSockets are not available. For example, it will fall back on JSON long polling in the absence of WebSocket support. Long polling is essentially a trick to emulate the WebSocket behavior in browsers that don't support WebSockets. After a long polling request is made, it is held onto by the server instead of immediately responding as a traditional HTTP request would. When data becomes available, the long polling request is resolved, closing the loop of the long request cycle. At this point, a new long polling request will typically be made. This gives the illusion of the continuous connection that WebSockets provides. Although long polling is less than ideal in the landscape of modern technology, it is a perfect fallback when needed. When you send a message with Socket.IO, the API for WebSockets and long polling are identical, so you don't have to deal with the mental overhead of integrating two syntactically different technologies.

Although there are Socket.IO implementations in many server-side languages, we will use Node.js in this book. With Node.js, we can write JavaScript on the server side, which gives us a single syntax on the server and client.

In this chapter, we will create a Node server with Socket.IO and obtain some very basic cross-browser messaging working. We will also look at debugging tools that make working with Socket.IO even easier.

Creating a Node HTTP server with Socket.IO

In order to get Socket.IO running, we need to have at least one client and one server set up to talk to each other. In this recipe, we will set up a basic Node HTTP server with the built-in Node `http` module.

Getting ready

To get started with Socket.IO, you will need to install Node.js. This can be downloaded from `https://nodejs.org/`.There is a download link on the Node.js website, or you can get one of the binaries at `https://nodejs.org/download/`.

Once Node.js is installed, you will need to navigate to the directory where your project is located and create a new NPM package by entering `npm init` in your console.

Now, you will need to install Socket.IO. You can use NPM to install Socket.IO by entering `npm install socket.io --save` on your terminal.

How to do it...

To create a Node HTTP server with Socket.IO, follow these steps:

1. Create a new file called `server.js`. This will be your server-side code:

```
var http = require('http'),
    socketIO = require('socket.io'),
    fs = require('fs'),
    server,
    io;

server = http.createServer(function (req, res) {
    fs.readFile(__dirname + '/index.html', function (err, data) {
      res.writeHead(200);
      res.end(data);
    });
});

server.listen(5000);
io = socketIO(server);

io.on('connection', function (socket) {
  socket.emit('greeting-from-server', {
      greeting: 'Hello Client'
  });
  socket.on('greeting-from-client', function (message) {
    console.log(message);
  });
});
```

2. You may see that `server.js` will read a file called `index.html`. You'll need to create this as well, as shown in the following code:

```
<!DOCTYPE html>
<html>
<head>
</head>
<body>
<script src="/socket.io/socket.io.js"></script>
<script>
            var socket = io('http://localhost:5000');
            socket.on('greeting-from-server', function
(message) {
```

```
                    document.body.appendChild(

document.createTextNode(message.greeting)
                    );
                    socket.emit('greeting-from-client', {
                        greeting: 'Hello Server'
                    });
                });
</script>
</body>
</html>
```

3. With your two files in place, you an start your server by entering `node server` on your terminal from the same directory where your files are. This will start a new Node server on port `5000`. Node can listen on any port, but we will specifically tell it to listen on port `5000` in our `server.js` file. If you navigate to `http://localhost:5000`, you should see a message that says **Hello Client** in your browser:

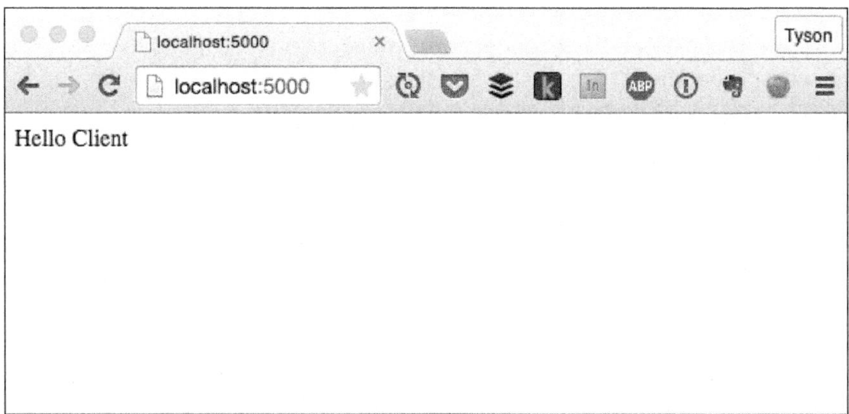

4. You should also see a message on your terminal with an object that contains a message that says **'Hello Server'**:

```
1. node
$ node server


{ greeting: 'Hello Server' }
```

Congratulations! Your client and your server are now talking to each other.

How it works...

The browser displays a message that originated on the server, whereas the server displays a message that originated on the client. These messages are both relayed by Socket.IO.

The client side also initializes a function, but in the client's case, we need to pass a string containing the server and port number if the server is not running on port `80`. In our case, we will run the server on port `5000`, so we need to pass `http://localhost:5000` in the io function.

The `/socket.io/socket.io.js` file is served dynamically by Socket.IO, so you don't need to manually add this file anywhere. As long as your server and Socket.IO are set up correctly, the script will be present. There is also a CDN available to host your `socket.io.js` file. The current version can be found at `http://socket.io/download`.

The `io.on('connection')` method in the server-side code listens for any new client-side socket connections. When the client loads a page with Socket.IO on the client side, a new connection will be created here.

When the server gets a new socket connection, it will emit a message to every available socket that says **Hello Client**. When the client gets this message, it will render it to the DOM. It also emits a message of its own that the server will listen for.

There's more...

Although all the examples in this book use Node.js on the server side, there are server-side libraries for many other languages, including, PHP, C#, Ruby, Python, and so on. Whatever your server-side language of choice happens to be, there is likely to be a library to interface with Socket.IO on your server.

Creating an Express server with Socket.IO

Express is probably the most widely used Node application framework available. Numerous MVC frameworks are written based on Express, but it can also be used on its own. Express is simple, flexible, and unopinionated, which makes it a pleasure to work with.

Socket.IO can be used based on the Express server just as easily as it can run on a standard Node HTTP server. In this section, we will fire the Express server and ensure that it can talk to the client side via Socket.IO.

Getting ready

The Express framework runs on Node, so you will need to have Node installed on your machine. Refer to the previous recipe for instructions on how to install Node and Socket.IO.

In addition to Node and Socket.IO, you will also need to install the Express npm package. Express can be installed by entering `npm install express --save` on your terminal.

How to do it...

Follow these steps to create an Express server using Socket.IO:

1. You will need to create a new server-side JavaScript file called `server.js`. It will contain all of your server instantiation and handle your Socket.IO messaging. The `server.js` file will look similar to the following code:

```
var express = require('express'),
    app = express(),
    http = require('http'),
    socketIO = require('socket.io'),
    server, io;

app.get('/', function (req, res) {
res.sendFile(__dirname + '/index.html');
});

server = http.Server(app);
server.listen(5000);

io = socketIO(server);

io.on('connection', function (socket) {
  socket.emit('greeting-from-server', {
      greeting: 'Hello Client'
  });
  socket.on('greeting-from-client', function (message) {
    console.log(message);
  });
});
```

2. The `server.js` file will serve a static HTML file called index when the user navigates to the root directory of the server. The HTML file will handle the client-side Socket.IO messaging. It will look similar to the following code:

```
<!DOCTYPE html>
<html>
<head>
</head>
<body>
<script src="/socket.io/socket.io.js"></script>
<script>
            var socket = io('http://localhost:5000');
            socket.on('greeting-from-server', function
(message) {
                document.body.appendChild(

document.createTextNode(message.greeting)
                );
                socket.emit('greeting-from-client', {
                    greeting: 'Hello Server'
                });
            });
</script>
</body>
</html>
```

3. Once both of your files are created, you can start your server by entering `node server` on your terminal.

4. After the server starts, you should be able to navigate to `http://localhost:5000` and see a message that says **Hello Client**:

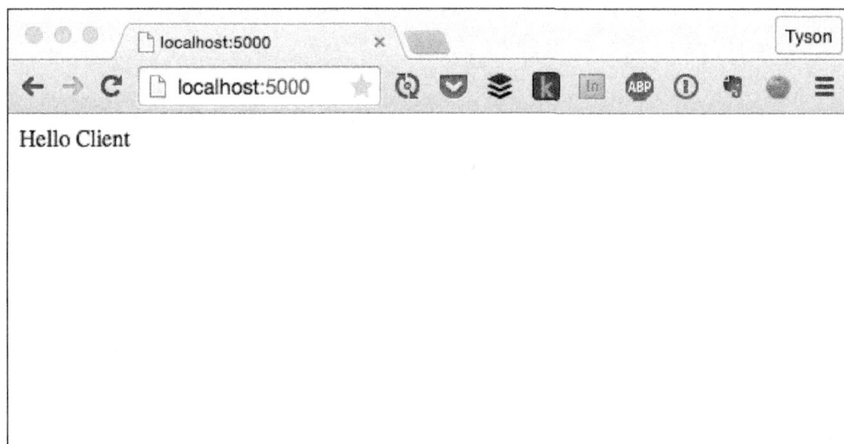

5. There should be a message that says **'Hello Server'** on your terminal:

```
1. node
$ node server

{ greeting: 'Hello Server' }
```

Awesome! Now you've got Socket.IO running on Express.

How it works...

Express is a collection of HTTP utilities and middleware that make it easier to use Node as a web server. Although Express provides a robust API that isn't available out of the box from the built-in Node HTTP module, using Express with Socket.IO is still very similar.

We created a new Express server with `var app = express()`. We passed this to the `http.Server()` method. By passing our Express app as the first argument to the HTTP server, we told Node that we wanted to use Express as our handler for HTTP requests.

Next, we passed the HTTP server directly to the `SocketIO` method exactly as we would have if we were using a nonExpress HTTP server. Socket.IO took the server instance to listen for new socket connections on it. The new connections came from the client side when we navigated to the page in our browser.

See also

Creating a Node HTTP server with Socket.IO.

Using Socket.IO as a cross-browser WebSocket

The native WebSocket implementation in browsers is much less robust than what Socket.IO offers. Sending a WebSocket message from the client only requires the data as a single argument. This means that you have to format your WebSocket data in such a way that you can easily determine what it is for.

If you want to emulate the ease of sending a message without a topic, you can use the `socket.send()` method to send messages as needed.

The benefits of using the Socket.IO syntax for this type of interaction over plain WebSockets are numerous. They include the built-in fallbacks for browsers that don't support WebSockets. The benefits also include a single unified syntax that is easier to read and maintain.

Getting ready

To get started with Socket.IO as a cross-browser WebSocket, you will need to have Node, Express, and Socket.IO installed. If you have not installed them yet, refer to the previous recipe: *Creating an Express server with Socket.IO*.

How to do it...

Follow these instructions to use Socket.IO as a cross-browser WebSocket:

1. First, you'll need to set up your server-side `server.js` file as follows:

```
var io = require('socket.io')(5000),
    sockets = [];

io.on('connection', function (socket) {
    sockets.push(socket);
    socket.on('message', function (message) {
        for (var i = 0; i < sockets.length; i++) {
            sockets[i].send(message);
        }
    });
    socket.on('disconnect', function () {
        console.log('The socket disconnected');
    });
});
```

2. Next, you'll have to create a client-side `index.html` file with the following code:

```
<!doctype html>
<html>
<head></head>
<body>
<form id="my-form">
<textarea id="message" placeholder="Message"></textarea>
<p>
<button type="submit">Send</button>
```

```
</p>
</form>

<div id="messages"></div>

<script
src="http://localhost:5000/socket.io/socket.io.js"></script
>
<script>
        var socket = io('http://localhost:5000');
        socket.on('connect', function () {

            document
                .getElementById('my-form')
                .addEventListener('submit', function (e) {
                   e.preventDefault();

socket.send(document.getElementById('message').value);
                });

            socket.on('message', function (message) {
                var messageNode =
document.createTextNode(message),
                    messageElement =
document.createElement('p');

                messageElement.appendChild(messageNode);


document.getElementById('messages').appendChild(messageElem
ent);
            });
        });
</script>
</body>
</html>
```

3. In our example, we have a simple form that allows the user to post a message that will be sent to all the connected sockets.

4. If you start your server with `node server` and open your `index.html` file by navigating to `http://5000/index.html` in your browser, you should see the form on the index page:

5. If you post a message to the form, it should send it to the server, and the server should broadcast it to all the available clients, as shown in the following screenshot:

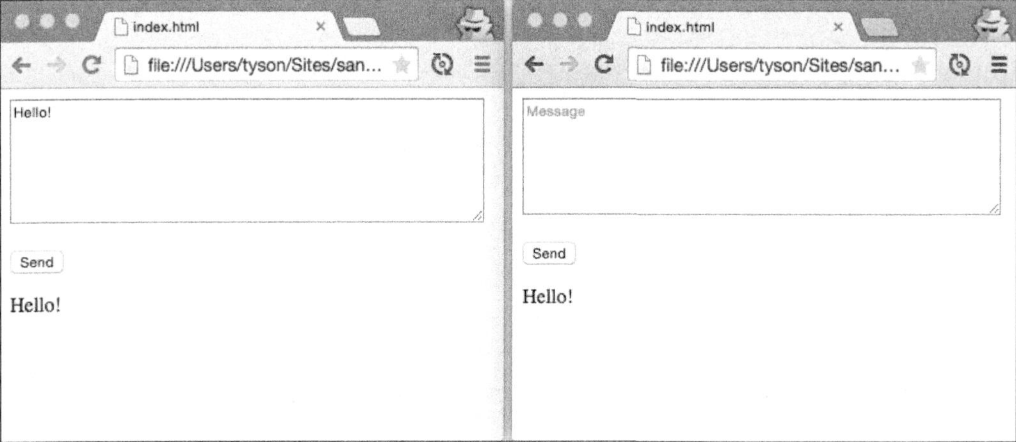

How it works...

The `socket.send(...)` method is a shortcut for `socket.emit('message', ...)`. We will take a look at this topic in *Chapter 3, Having Two-Way Conversations*. This is the reason when the server listens for a message topic, it gets called when the client calls `socket.send()`.

Our server stores an array of all the topics that connect to it. We will loop through all the connected sockets to send the message when it comes. We will also explore better ways to manage the connected sockets in the next chapter.

The client side aids the duty of sending the data from the form to the server. It also listens for new messages from the server to add to the list of available messages in our UI underneath the form.

There's more...

We will keep an array of all the connected sockets so that we will be able to easily send data to all of them as needed. However, keeping an array of all the connected sockets can be a little more tedious than just pushing the sockets to the array when they connect. For example, if a user leaves the page, the socket will disconnect, but it will still be included in the static array.

Fortunately, we will be able to tap into the socket disconnect event by calling `socket.on('disconnect')`. Using this method, we can remove the socket from our array and avoid sending messages to an abandoned socket connection.

Here is an example of how the disconnect event can be used to manage dropped connections:

```
var io = require('socket.io')(5000),
    sockets = [];

io.on('connection', function (socket) {
    sockets.push(socket);
    socket.on('disconnect', function () {
        for (var i = 0; i < sockets.length; i++) {
            if (sockets[i].id === socket.id) {
                sockets .splice(i, 1);
            }
        }
        console.log('The socket disconnected. There are ' +
sockets.length + ' connected sockets');
    });
});
```

See also

- The *Handling connection timeouts* section in *Chapter 2, Creating Real-Time Dashboards*
- The *Creating a simple chat room* section in *Chapter 3, Having Two-Way Conversations*.

Debugging on the client

In the earlier versions of Socket.IO, debugging was extremely simple. This was because verbose logging was pushed to the developer console by default. Although this feature was a great way to dig into issues when they occurred, it could also get in the way by logging too much when no debugging was needed.

Now, Socket.IO gives us the ability to toggle certain parts of our logging on and off as needed. In this recipe, we will enable client-side debugging to have a better view of what is happening in our Socket.IO communication.

Getting ready

Starting with version 1.0, Socket.IO doesn't show any logging by default. However, it can easily be turned on. Behind the scenes, it will use an NPM module called `debug`, which allows logging to navigate to various scopes that can be turned on or off as needed.

How to do it...

To enable debugging on the client side, follow these steps:

1. On the client side, log settings are persisted through HTML5 `localStorage`, so you can turn logging on by setting the value of `localStorage.debug`.
2. To see all the logging messages, just set the value of debug to an asterisk, as shown in the following code:

   ```
   localStorage.debug = '*';
   ```

3. Now that robust logging is turned on, you can open your developer tools and see a rich array of messages that details what is happening under the hood:

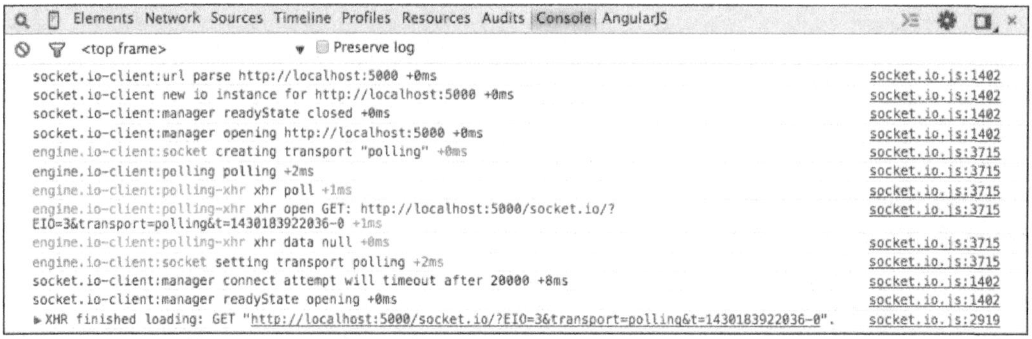

```
Elements Network Sources Timeline Profiles Resources Audits Console AngularJS
<top frame>  Preserve log
socket.io-client:url parse http://localhost:5000 +0ms                                  socket.io.js:1402
socket.io-client new io instance for http://localhost:5000 +0ms                        socket.io.js:1402
socket.io-client:manager readyState closed +0ms                                        socket.io.js:1402
socket.io-client:manager opening http://localhost:5000 +0ms                            socket.io.js:1402
engine.io-client:socket creating transport "polling" +0ms                              socket.io.js:3715
engine.io-client:polling polling +2ms                                                  socket.io.js:3715
engine.io-client:polling-xhr xhr poll +1ms                                             socket.io.js:3715
engine.io-client:polling-xhr xhr open GET: http://localhost:5000/socket.io/?           socket.io.js:3715
EIO=3&transport=polling&t=1430183922036-0 +1ms
engine.io-client:polling-xhr xhr data null +0ms                                        socket.io.js:3715
engine.io-client:socket setting transport polling +2ms                                 socket.io.js:3715
socket.io-client:manager connect attempt will timeout after 20000 +8ms                 socket.io.js:1402
socket.io-client:manager readyState opening +0ms                                       socket.io.js:1402
▶XHR finished loading: GET "http://localhost:5000/socket.io/?EIO=3&transport=polling&t=1430183922036-0".   socket.io.js:2919
```

How it works...

The `localStorage` object in the browser is an object with key/value pairs that is maintained when you refresh the page or leave it entirely. It is useful for persisting data on the client side in modern browsers.

Socket.IO uses the debug NPM module. This views the `localStorage` key to determine the logging level to be displayed in the browser. The fact that the debugging level is set in `localStorage` can be very useful because you can set a debugging type anywhere even in production, and it will only log on to your machine. Also, you will be able to refresh the page and see the Socket.IO logging from the initial page load, which can be really handy for debugging events that occur earlier on the page life cycle.

There's more...

Not only can you set the logging to show everything, you can also listen for only certain log types by setting them up in `localStorage`. For example, if you are only interested in XHR requests, you can ask to only see messages in the `engine.io-client:polling-xhr` namespace with the following code:

```
localStorage.debug = 'engine.io-client:polling-xhr';
```

You can also set multiple log types by separating them with a comma, as shown in the following code:

```
localStorage.debug = 'engine.io-client:polling, engine.io-
client:socket';
```

See also

The following recipe, *Debugging on the server*.

Debugging on the server

The same debugging package that is available on the client side is available on the server as well.

The debugging option can be turned on with a Node environmental variable.

Getting ready

To get started with debugging on the server side, you will need to have Node and Socket.IO installed and an existing app that uses Socket.IO. To test this out, you can easily use any of the apps we built in the previous recipes in this chapter.

How to do it...

To get server-side debugging turned on, follow these steps:

1. To enable debugging at the time when you start your server, simply include the `DEBUG` environmental variable as the first argument when you start your Node server, as shown in the following code:

   ```
   DEBUG=* node server
   ```

2. If you would like to persist the `DEBUG` environmental variable without the need to pass it every time you start your Node server, you can export it ahead of time using the following code:

   ```
   export  DEBUG=*
   ```

3. Now, when you start your server, verbose logging will be used with the following code:

   ```
   node server
   ```

4. You can always update the `DEBUG` variable or even remove it completely by setting it to null, which will suppress logging entirely, as shown in the following code:

   ```
   export DEBUG=null
   ```

How it works...

Node.js environmental variables are available in `process.env` in any running Node process. They are often used to set up server-specific configurations, such as database connections and third-party credentials.

The great thing about using environmental variables to define the logging verbosity is that most cloud-based hosting providers allow you to change environmental variables on the fly, so you can easily toggle logging on or off without having to redeploy your code.

There's more...

Similar to client-side logging, you can set the logging type to something other than the wildcard. This allows you to only get debugging messages on the topic you want to listen to.

For example, listening for XHR requests is as simple as passing it to the environmental variables when you start your Node server with the following code:

```
DEBUG=socket.io:server node server
```

2

Creating Real-Time Dashboards

In this chapter, we will cover the following recipes:

- Loading static data from the server
- Creating a server-side clock
- Loading data from MongoDB
- Real-time analytics
- Handling connection timeouts

Introduction

Although there is a great deal of power in bidirectional communication, Socket.IO is also a perfect tool for creating unidirectional real-time experiences. Many applications need to have some sort of dashboard interface to display analytical data or to show the state of the application data. For an application state that frequently changes, or if there are multiple users changing the state, creating the dashboard in real time makes for a much better experience.

In this chapter, we will implement various techniques to display and maintain real-time dashboards that only harness a unidirectional data flow in order to pass data from the server to the client.

Loading static data from the server

In order to understand how Socket.IO pushes data to the client, we will create an application that emits a static object. Although this exercise may seem contrived, the only difference between static data and dynamic data is that static data only needs to be emitted once, whereas dynamic data needs to be emitted on each mutation. The client side doesn't concern itself with the frequency of state changes, so the difference between emitting data once and emitting data frequently is inconsequential. If we can rerender the state of a dashboard once, we can rerender it a million times.

Once we've completed this recipe, our dashboard will look similar to the following screenshot:

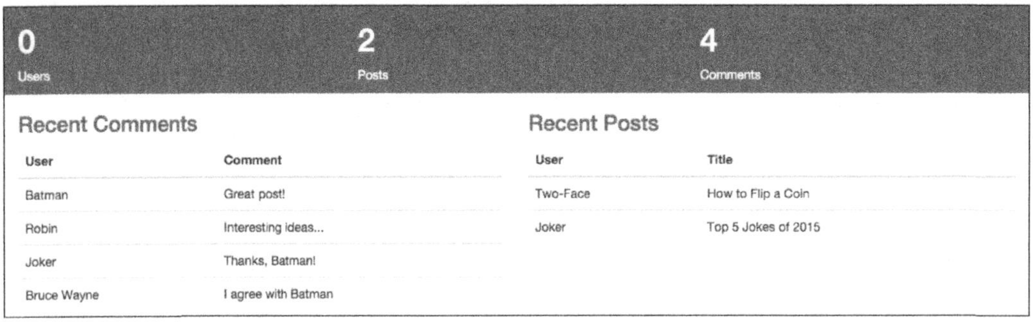

0	2	4
Users	Posts	Comments

Recent Comments

User	Comment
Batman	Great post!
Robin	Interesting ideas...
Joker	Thanks, Batman!
Bruce Wayne	I agree with Batman

Recent Posts

User	Title
Two-Face	How to Flip a Coin
Joker	Top 5 Jokes of 2015

Getting ready

In addition to Socket.IO and Node, we will use Express for this exercise. Make sure that you have installed Express by running `npm install express socket.io` on your terminal.

How to do it...

To load static data with Socket.IO, follow these steps:

1. Create your `server.js` Node file. This will be responsible for starting up your server, setting up Socket.IO, and instantiating your individual socket controllers, as shown in the following code:

```
var express = require('express'),
    app = express(),
    http = require('http'),
    socketIO = require('socket.io'),
    server, io;

app.get('/', function (req, res) {
```

```
        res.sendFile(__dirname + '/index.html');
    });

    server = http.Server(app);
    server.listen(5000);

    io = socketIO(server);

    io.on('connection', function (socket) {
        var controllers = ['comments', 'posts'];
        for (var i = 0; i<controllers.length; i++) {
            require('./controllers/' + controllers[i] +
    '.controller')(socket);
        }
    });
```

2. Now, create your `comments controller` file. This file should reside in `controller/comments.controller.js`. It will loop through all of our comments and emit a `comments.add` event that the client can listen for in order to display users in the dashboard. It will also emit a `comments.count` event for each comment in your static array with the following code:

```
var comments = [{
    user: 'Batman',
    comment: 'Great post!'
}, {
    user: 'Robin',
    comment: 'Interesting ideas...'
}, {
    user: 'Joker',
    comment: 'Thanks, Batman!'
}, {
    user: 'Bruce Wayne',
    comment: 'I agree with Batman'
}];

module.exports = function (socket) {

    // Recent Comments
    for (var i = 0; i<comments.length; i++) {
        socket.emit('comment.add', comments[i]);
        socket.emit('comments.count', {
            count: i + 1
        });
    }


};
```

3. Then, you can create your posts controller. This is very similar to our comments controller. It loops through a static array of posts and emits an event to add the post. It also emits an event to update the posts count, as shown in the following code:

```
var posts = [{
    user: 'Two-Face',
    title: 'How to Flip a Coin'
}, {
    user: 'Joker',
    title: 'Top 5 Jokes of 2015'
}];

module.exports = function (socket) {

    // Recent Posts
    for (var i = 0; i<posts.length; i++) {
        socket.emit('post.add', posts[i]);
        socket.emit('posts.count', {
            count: i + 1
        });
    }

};
```

4. Now that our server-side code is ready, we need to create our client-side template to render our data when it is available. We'll use Bootstrap to style the page and make it look nice. The markup will look similar to the following code:

```
<link rel="stylesheet"
href="https://maxcdn.bootstrapcdn.com/bootstrap/3.3.4/css/b
ootstrap.min.css" />
<div class="container">
    <div class="row bg-primary">
        <div class="col-md-4">
            <h1 id="users-count">0</h1>
            <p>Users</p>
        </div>
        <div class="col-md-4">
            <h1 id="posts-count">0</h1>
            <p>Posts</p>
        </div>
        <div class="col-md-4">
            <h1 id="comments-count">0</h1>
            <p>Comments</p>
        </div>
    </div>
```

```
    <div class="row">
        <div class="col-md-6">
            <h3 class="text-primary">Recent Comments</h3>
            <table class="table">
                <thead>
                    <tr>
                        <th>User</th>
                        <th>Comment</th>
                    </tr>
                </thead>
                <tbody id="recent-comments">
                    <!-- Recent Comments -->
                </tbody>
            </table>
        </div>
        <div class="col-md-6">
            <h3 class="text-primary">Recent Posts</h3>
            <table class="table">
                <thead>
                    <tr>
                        <th>User</th>
                        <th>Title</th>
                    </tr>
                </thead>
                <tbody id="recent-posts">
                    <!-- Recent Posts -->
                </tbody>
            </table>
        </div>
    <div>
</div>
<script src="http://code.jquery.com/jquery-
2.1.4.min.js"></script>
<script src="/socket.io/socket.io.js"></script>
```

5. Lastly, we need to add the client-side Socket.IO event listeners. They can either go directly in the `index.html` file or they may be included as an external resource. They will listen for posts and comments and then render them to the page. We will use jQuery for simplicity, but you could easily use any other client-side framework if you need more structure, as shown in the following code:

```
var socket = io('http://localhost:5000');

// Update the users count
socket.on('users.count', function (data) {
```

```
        $('#users-count').text(data.count);
    });

    // Update the comments count
    socket.on('comments.count', function (data) {
        $('#comments-count').text(data.count);
    });

    // Updae the posts count
    socket.on('posts.count', function (data) {
        $('#posts-count').text(data.count);
    });

    // Add a comment
    socket.on('comment.add', function (data) {
        var $row = $('<tr>' +
            '<td>' + data.user + '</td>' +
            '<td>' + data.comment + '</td>' +
        '</tr>');
        $('#recent-comments').append($row);
    });

    // Add a post
    socket.on('post.add', function (data) {
        var $row = $('<tr>' +
            '<td>' + data.user + '</td>' +
            '<td>' + data.title + '</td>' +
        '</tr>');
        $('#recent-posts').append($row);
    });
```

How it works...

Our server will include the comments and posts controllers. These controllers will emit the static arrays as soon as they are initialized. We will emit the records one at a time, so we could easily emit more data (one row at a time) if we switched from using static data to using real dynamic data.

There's more...

As we will be emitting our records individually, they don't have to be emitted all at once. For another contrived example, we could send our posts one at a time every two seconds. This can be achieved by amending the end of our `posts.controller` file to something similar to the following code:

```
var i = 0;
var addingPosts = setInterval(function () {
    if (posts[i]) {
        socket.emit('post.add', posts[i]);
        socket.emit('posts.count', {
            count: i + 1
        });
        i++;
    } else {
        clearInterval(addingPosts);
    }
}, 2000);
```

Creating a server-side clock

It is sometimes useful to have the date and time from the server side instead of the client side. We're usually interested in the client-side time zone, but this isn't always the case. For example, if we create a dashboard for a web-hosting platform, it could be helpful to display the time as it appears on the server.

In this recipe, we will create a server-side clock that updates the user interface in real time so that we always know what time the server thinks it is.

How to do it...

To create a server-side clock that emits data to the client-side, follow these steps:

1. First, create a `server.js` file that emits a new date string every second. To do this, we will set an interval of `1000` ms and emit `new Date()` for this interval. In JavaScript, when we create `new Date()` with no arguments, it will always be set to the current date and time, as shown in the following code:

    ```
    var express = require('express'),
        app = express(),
        http = require('http'),
        socketIO = require('socket.io'),
    ```

```
    server, io;

app.get('/', function (req, res) {
    res.sendFile(__dirname + '/index.html');
});

server = http.Server(app);
server.listen(5000);

io = socketIO(server);

io.on('connection', function (socket) {
    setInterval(function () {
        socket.emit('seconds.update', {
            time: new Date()
        });
    }, 1000);
});
```

2. Now we need to add some client-side code to render the date when it is available. The date object that the server side sends will automatically be converted to a string before it is sent, so we will need to cast it back to a date object so that it can be displayed in a human-readable format, as shown in the following code:

```
<link rel="stylesheet"
href="https://maxcdn.bootstrapcdn.com/bootstrap/3.3.4/css/b
ootstrap.min.css" />
<div class="container">
    <div class="row bg-primary">
        <div class="col-md-12">
            <h1></h1>
        </div>
    </div>
</div>
<script src="http://code.jquery.com/jquery-
2.1.4.min.js"></script>
<script src="/socket.io/socket.io.js"></script>
<script>
    var socket = io('http://localhost:5000');
    socket.on('seconds.update', function (data) {
        var time = new Date(data.time);
        $('h1').text(
            time.getMonth() + '\/' + time.getDate() + '\/'
+ time.getFullYear() + ' ' +
```

```
                time.getHours() + ':' + time.getMinutes() + ':'
+ time.getSeconds());
    });
</script>
```

3. We should now be able to navigate to our page and see a clock that updates every second

How it works...

The server-side date may be different from the client-side date if the server and the client are in different time zones. We will be able to get around this by emitting the server-side date to the client. By emitting a new date each second, the clock interface will always be accurate.

Loading data from MongoDB

As we are now able to send static data to our client with Socket.IO, we have all the tools we need to send dynamic data as well. MongoDB is a NoSQL database that stores data as JSON documents. In this recipe, we will send data from our database to the client side to get rendered.

Getting ready

Before you begin, you will need to install MongoDB on your machine. MongoDB can be installed by navigating to `https://www.mongodb.org` and following the installation steps there. Once MongoDB is installed, you can start the MongoDB server by entering `mongod` on your terminal window. Leave the `mongod` process running; you'll need to have it available to access your database.

You will also have to install a Node adapter for MongoDB. We will use Mongoose. This can be installed from NPM by entering `npm install mongoose` on your terminal.

How to do it...

To send dynamic data from a MongoDB database via Socket.IO, follow these steps:

1. First, we will create a `server.js` file. This will be the file that starts the server and loads all of our server-side dependencies:

```
var express = require('express'),
    app = express(),
    http = require('http'),
    socketIO = require('socket.io'),
```

```
    server, io;

app.get('/', function (req, res) {
    res.sendFile(__dirname + '/index.html');
});

server = http.Server(app);
server.listen(5000);

io = socketIO(server);

io.on('connection', function (socket) {
    var controllers = ['comments', 'posts'];
    for (var i = 0; i < controllers.length; i++) {
        require('./controllers/' + controllers[i] +
'.controller')(socket);
    }
});
```

2. We will import a file from `lib/mongo.js`. This file will simply connect to a MongoDB database and export the `mongoose` instance for us to use throughout the app.

```
var mongoose = require('mongoose');
mongoose.connect('mongodb://localhost/dashboard');
module.exports = mongoose;
```

3. Now, we will need to include a MongoDB model for our comments. This can go in `models/comment.js`. This file will be responsible for creating a schema for our model and then returning the model itself, as shown in the following code:

```
var mongoose = require('../lib/mongo');

var commentSchema = mongoose.Schema({
    user: String,
    comment: String
});

module.exports = mongoose.model('Comment', commentSchema);
```

4. Now that we have a comments model, we can access it in our `controllers/comments.controller.js` file with the following code:

```
var Comment = require('../models/comment');

module.exports = function (socket) {
```

```
    var stream = Comment.find().stream();

    stream.on('data', function (comment) {
        socket.emit('comment.add', comment);
    });
};
```

5. Then, we need to create our `index.html` template. This will listen for any new comments from the server and append them to the DOM, as shown in the following code:

```
<link rel="stylesheet"
href="https://maxcdn.bootstrapcdn.com/bootstrap/3.3.4/css/b
ootstrap.min.css" />
<div class="container">
    <div class="row">
        <div class="col-md-12">
            <h3 class="text-primary">Recent Comments</h3>
            <table class="table">
                <thead>
                    <tr>
                        <th>User</th>
                        <th>Comment</th>
                    </tr>
                </thead>
                <tbody id="recent-comments">
                    <!-- Recent Comments -->
                </tbody>
            </table>
        </div>
    <div>
</div>
<script src="http://code.jquery.com/jquery-
2.1.4.min.js"></script>
<script src="/socket.io/socket.io.js"></script>
<script>
    var socket = io('http://localhost:5000');

    // Add a comment
    socket.on('comment.add', function (data) {
        var $row = $('<tr>' +
            '<td>' + data.user + '</td>' +
            '<td>' + data.comment + '</td>' +
        '</tr>');
        $('#recent-comments').append($row);
    });
</script>
```

6. Finally, we need to display data in our dashboard. We can create a `lib/seed.js` file to handle seeding and call it by running node `lib/seed` on the terminal:

```
var Comment = require('../models/comment');

// New comments
var comments = [{
    user: 'Batman',
    comment: 'Great post!'
}, {
    user: 'Robin',
    comment: 'Interesting ideas...'
}, {
    user: 'Joker',
    comment: 'Thanks, Batman!'
}, {
    user: 'Bruce Wayne',
    comment: 'I agree with Batman'
}];

// Loop over new comments and create them
for (var i = 0; i < comments.length; i++) {
    new Comment(comments[i]).save();
}

console.log('Database Seeded');

process.exit(0);
```

How it works...

We will use the Mongoose stream method in our controller by calling `Comment.find().stream()`. Using the stream method, we will be able to pipe our comments to Socket.IO one by one as and when they are available.

What we are doing is not much different from just piping in static data. The only difference is that we are listening to the database stream to pipe the data from.

Real-time analytics

Socket.IO excels at creating rich real-time analytic dashboards. In this recipe, we will display the count of users currently on our page, but the same concept could be used to show much more detailed analytical data if it is provided.

How to do it...

To show a real-time count of the users currently on a page, follow these steps:

1. Create a `server.js` file that emits the count of active users on the page whenever the count changes. Take a look at the following code:

```
var express = require('express'),
    app = express(),
    http = require('http'),
    socketIO = require('socket.io'),
    server, io;

app.get('/', function (req, res) {
    res.sendFile(__dirname + '/index.html');
});

server = http.Server(app);
server.listen(5000);

io = socketIO(server);

var count = 0;

io.on('connection', function (socket) {
    count++;
    io.emit('users.count', count);
    socket.on('disconnect', function () {
        count--;
        io.emit('users.count', count);
    });
});
```

2. Now, display the results in the `index.html` template, as shown in the following code:

```
<!DOCTYPE html>
<html>
    <head></head>
    <body>
        <h1 id="users-count">?</h1>
        <p>Active Users On This Page</p>
        <script src="/socket.io/socket.io.js"></script>
        <script>
            var socket = io('http://localhost:5000');
```

```
                socket.on('users.count', function (number) {
                    document.getElementById('users-count').innerHTML =
number;
                });
            </script>
        </body>
    </html>
```

3. To test this, open this page in a few different browser windows. Every time you add or remove a browser window, the count of active users will change.

How it works...

On the server, we will keep a variable with the number of currently connected sockets. We will emit an event every time the count changes. This allows you to always have the ability to display the number of current users on this page.

There's more...

To display real-time data with more detailed information, you would need to emit a custom event from the client instead of just listening for a socket connection. The custom event would include any information that you could only get from the browser. It may contain the browser and demographic information that isn't available on the server. Here is an example of a slightly richer analytics tracking:

```
socket.emit('analytics.log', {
    userAgent: window.navigator.userAgent,
    location: window.location,
    track: !window.navigator.doNotTrack
});
```

Handling connection timeouts

When we perform a real-time application development, it is important to be aware of when the server-side WebSocket connection is dropped, and we will no longer be able to communicate with our server. This allows you to provide an offline mode for our apps, where we can keep a record of all the events that need to be emitted to the server once the connection is re-established.

Socket.IO has some really great built-in functionalities to re-establish the connection once it has been dropped. This is accomplished by creating recurring polling requests to the server until a new connection is found or until the number of reconnection attempts we allow are exceeded.

Getting ready

For this recipe, we will use Express to serve our Socket.IO application. Most of the magic in this recipe will take place on the client side, so the server is really not as important as long as it is a functional server that hosts Socket.IO.

How to do it...

To handle connection timeouts in Socket.IO, follow these steps:

1. First, we will create a basic server that spawns a Socket.IO connection.

```
var express = require('express'),
    app = express(),
    http = require('http'),
    socketIO = require('socket.io'),
    server, io;

app.get('/', function (req, res) {
    res.sendFile(__dirname + '/index.html');
});

server = http.Server(app);
server.listen(5000);

io = socketIO(server);
```

2. All the connection timeout handling will happen on the client side. Socket.IO gives us several socket life cycle events that we can tap into. We can use these events to know when we lose a connection, when we successfully reconnect, and so on. We will use the lifecycle callbacks in our template to listen for socket reconnections.

```
<!DOCTYPE html>
<html>
    <head></head>
    <body>
        <p>Open up your developer console, kill your server
and let the fun begin!</p>
        <script src="/socket.io/socket.io.js"></script>
        <script>
            var socket = io('http://localhost:5000', {
                'reconnection': true,
                'reconnectionDelay': 500,
                'reconnectionAttempts': 5
            });
```

```
            socket.on('reconnect', function (number) {
                console.info('After attempting ' + number +
' times, we finally reconnected!');
            });

            socket.on('reconnect_attempt', function
(number) {
                console.info('Reconnect attempt number ' +
number);
            });

            socket.on('connect_error', function () {
                console.warn('Error connecting to
Socket.IO');
            });

            socket.on('reconnect_failed', function () {
                console.error('We failed to reconnect to
Socket.IO. We give up.');
            });
        </script>
    </body>
</html>
```

3. Finally, start your server, navigate to the page in your browser, and kill your server to simulate a connection from being dropped. You may also want to set `localStorage.debug = '*';` on your console so that you can see the debugging information. This verifies that the socket connection has been dropped as expected.

How it works...

We will be able to pass an object of options as our second argument when we call the `io()` function on the client side.

By default, the `reconnection` option is set to `true`. If we set `reconnection` to `false`, Socket.IO will not attempt to reconnect when a connection is dropped.

The `reconnectionDelay` option specifies how many milliseconds are allowed to pass before we ping the server for a reconnection. The pinging will continue to take place until the number of `reconnectionAttempts` we specified is satisfied or until the connection is re-established. By default, the reconnection attempts are set to `Infinity`.

3

Having Two-Way Conversations

In this chapter, we will cover the following recipes:

- Creating a simple chat room
- Managing the socket life cycle
- Emitting a private message to another socket
- Sending messages to all the sockets, except for the sender
- Building a multiplayer tic-tac-toe game

Introduction

Although we can perform some interesting things with one-way communication, the real power of Socket.IO begins to show when the client and server are both participants in a constant dialog.

In this chapter, we will work through various examples of two-way Socket.IO communication. We will implement various tactics to make bidirectional communication work for our specific needs.

Creating a simple chat room

A basic chat room application is one of the most widely used demos. This shows off Socket.IO or even web sockets in a more general sense. The reason for this is that it immediately gives the business case for Socket.IO in a way that is easy to follow and digest.

Building a basic chat room with Socket.IO is neither terribly difficult or complex. This is the sort of application that Socket.IO was designed for.

When we have completed our chat application, it will look something similar to the following screenshot:

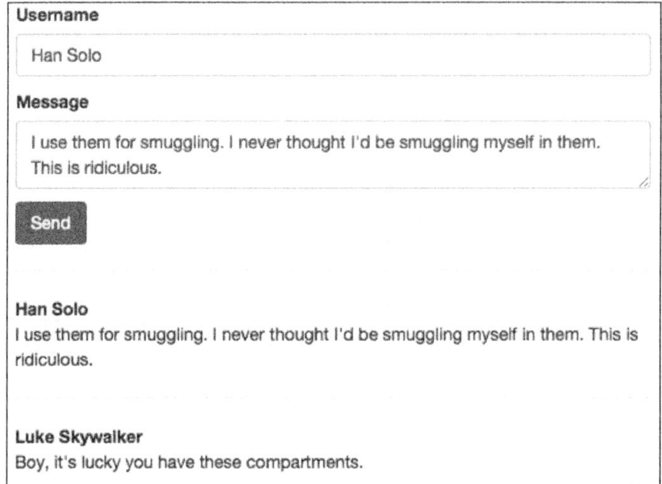

Getting ready

For this recipe, we will use jQuery for simple DOM manipulation and Bootstrap for styling purposes. None of these libraries are required to create a chat app with Socket.IO, but they all provide useful utilities that we can easily tap into.

How to do it...

To create a simple chat application with Socket.IO, follow these steps:

1. Create a `server.js` file. This file will start your server and emit Socket.IO events whenever a new message is posted to the chat application. In addition to the typical Socket.IO server setup, we will need to add the following code:

```
io.on('connection', function (socket) {
    socket.on('message.send', function (data) {
        io.emit('message.sent', data);
    });
});
```

2. Now, create your `index.html` template. This will include a form at the top of the page to post new messages. It also contains a `div` container to hold our chat messages:

```
<div class="container">
    <form id="message-form">
        <p>
             <label>Username</label>
             <input class="form-control" id="username" />
        </p>
        <p>
            <label>Message</label>
            <textarea class="form-control"
id="message"></textarea>
        </p>
        <button class="btnbtn-primary"
type="submit">Send</button>
    </form>
    <div id="messages"></div>
</div>
```

3. Then, add the client-side JavaScript. This will submit messages to the server and render messages when they are emitted from the server, as shown in the following code:

```
// Update the users count
socket.on('message.sent', function (data) {
    $('#messages').prepend(`
<div>
    <hr />
    <div><strong>${data.username}</strong></div>
    <p>${data.message}</p>
</div>
    `);
});

$(function () {
    $('#message-form').on('submit', function (e) {
        e.preventDefault();
        socket.emit('message.send', {
            message: $('#message').val(),
            username: $('#username').val()
        });
    });
});
```

How it works...

The server-side code will act as a hub for incoming messages. When new messages come, it will emit them to all connected sockets.

We will submit the messages from our form on the client side. We will also render new messages when they are emitted from the server. In this way, the client who emits the message will listen for the same `message.sent` event, as all the other clients.

There's more...

The messages in this simple example will not be persisted. This means that when the client first loads the page, there will not be any messages in the interface. They will only receive messages when new messages are posted after the page is loaded.

To show all the messages that occurred before the page load, we would need to maintain them somehow and emit them when the socket `connection` event is fired on the server.

For example, we could hold an array of posted messages in the memory and emit them when the page is loaded. The downside to the in-memory approach is that when the server is restarted, all the messages that we previously had in the memory would be lost.

A better approach would be to keep the messages in a database and fetch the previously posted messages when the connection is created.

Managing the socket life cycle

If our server maintains a list of our connected sockets, it should always be mindful of when a socket disconnects.

A socket can disconnect for any number of reasons:

- The user may navigate away from the web page that the WebSocket connection is on
- The user's Internet may go down

When these things happen, we can tap into the `disconnect` event to notify the client side that the socket is no longer available.

How to do it...

To remove references from disconnected sockets, follow these steps:

1. First, listen for the socket `disconnect` event on the server side. When this occurs, we will emit an event back to the clients with the ID of the socket that was disconnected. Socket.IO associates every socket with a unique ID, which we can use to manage our sockets. Here is the server-side code:

```
io.on('connection', function (socket) {
io.emit('user.add', socket.id);

socket.on('disconnect', function () {
io.emit('user.remove', socket.id)
    });
});
```

2. Then, add an element to your view that contains the list of users:

```
<div id="users"></div>
```

3. Finally, in the client, we will listen to the `user.add` and `user.remove` events to add or remove users as they are connected or disconnected:

```
socket.on('user.add', function (id) {
    $('#users').prepend(`<p id="${id}">${id}</p>`);
});

socket.on('user.remove', function (id) {
    $(`#${id}`).remove();
});
```

How it works...

Although the ID of a socket is primarily available for internal use, when we manage a list of connected users, it can be beneficial to have a record of the socket IDs to associate it with the rendered list in our interface.

In our case, we will use the socket ID as the actual `id` attribute for our DOM elements. The ID will look similar to a random assortment of numbers and letters (such as `AL8r1DvmiQVT50trAAAC`). By using the socket ID in tandem with the socket life cycle events, we will be able to show the list of currently active users on the page.

Emitting a private message to another socket

Sometimes, you need to send a private message to just one other socket and not every socket that may be listening in. As the server side is in charge of managing all the connected sockets, we can specify the sockets that our events are emitted to granularly.

In this recipe, we will use this ability to create a simple app. Here, the user can specify which user to give a hug to. Only the giver and receiver will be aware that the hug was initiated. Our application will look something similar to the following screenshot:

Getting ready

For this recipe, we will use jQuery for the DOM manipulation and Bootstrap for styling purposes.

How to do it...

To send private messages using Socket.IO, follow these steps:

1. Add the relevant events to your server. These will be in charge of managing a list of connected users and emitting private messages to users (as required). In addition to the typical Socket.IO server-side setup, you will require the following code:

```
// We will keep a record of all connected sockets
var sockets = {};

io.on('connection', function (socket) {

    // Emit the connected users when a new socket connects
for (vari in sockets) {
```

```
socket.emit('user.add', {
username: sockets[i].username,
id: sockets[i].id
        });
    }

    // Add a new user
socket.on('username.create', function (data) {
socket.username = data;
sockets[socket.id] = socket;
io.emit('user.add', {
username: socket.username,
id: socket.id
        });
    });

    // Send the hug event to only the socket specified
socket.on('user.hug', function (id) {
sockets[id].emit('user.hugged', socket.username);
    });

    // Remove disconnected users
socket.on('disconnect', function () {
delete sockets[socket.id];
io.emit('user.remove', socket.id);
    });
});
```

2. Now, create a `index.html` template to display the interface for your application:

```
<div class="container">

<h1><span class="glyphiconglyphicon-heart"></span> Hugs!</h1>

<hr />

<form id="add-username" class="row">
<div class="col-md-3">
<input class="form-control" id="username"
placeholder="Username" />
</div>
<div class="col-md-3">
<button class="btnbtn-primary">Join</button>
</div>
```

```
</form>

<div class="row">
<div class="col-md-6" id="sockets" style="display:
none"></div>
<div class="col-md-6" id="hugs"></div>
</div>

</div>
```

3. Then, add listeners to the client side in order to display the users. Also, keep a log of the private messages that have been emitted with the following code:

```
function addUser (user) {
    $('#sockets').append(`
        <div id="${user.id}" class="socket">
        <span class="glyphicon-user"></span>
        ${user.username} -
    <a href="#" class="hug" data-
username="${user.username}" data-id="${user.id}">Hug</a>
    <hr />
    </div>
`);
}

function addUsername (e) {
    e.preventDefault();

    socket.emit('username.create', $('#username').val());
    $('#sockets').show();
    $(this).hide();
}

function giveHug (e) {

var id = $(this).data('id'),
      username = $(this).data('username');

e.preventDefault();

socket.emit('user.hug', id);

    $('#hugs').prepend(`
        <p>
```

```
        <span class="glyphiconglyphicon-heart-
empty"></span>
            You just hugged ${username}.
        <hr />
        </p>
`);
}

socket.on('users.list', function (list) {
list.forEach(addUser);
});

socket.on('user.hugged', function (username) {
    $('#hugs').prepend(`
        <p>
            <span class="glyphiconglyphicon-heart"></span>
        ${username} just hugged you.
<hr />
</p>
`);
});

socket.on('user.remove', function (id) {
    $('#' + id).remove();
});

socket.on('user.add', addUser);

$(function () {
    $('#sockets').delegate('.hug', 'click', giveHug);
    $('#add-username').on('submit', addUsername);
});
```

How it works...

By maintaining a list of available sockets in our server-side object, we will be able to search for any socket by its ID. When we have the socket that we want to send a private message to, we can emit an event to only this socket and no others.

Sending messages to all the sockets, except for the sender

When a socket sends a message, we don't necessarily want it to receive the message that it sent. We may want to display a different message to the sender than to the receivers. This can be accomplished using the `socket.broadcast.emit()` syntax.

How to do it...

To send messages to every socket, except for the sender, follow these steps:

1. First, create a template for sockets to announce their presence. This will also include a `"messages"` container. Here, we will render incoming messages:

```
<div class="container">
<hr />
<form id="form" class="row">
<div class="col-md-10">
<input class="form-control" id="name" placeholder="Who are
you?" />
</div>
<div class="col-md-2">
<button class="btn-primary form-control"
type="submit">Send</button>
</div>
</form>
<div id="messages"></div>
</div>
```

2. Then, add some client-side JavaScript to render messages, as shown in the following code:

```
socket.on('user.joined', function (data) {
    $('#messages').prepend(`
<p>
<hr />
            ${data.name} is finally here.
</p>
    `);
});

$(function () {
    $('#form').on('submit', function (e) {
```

```
e.preventDefault();

var name = $('#name').val();

socket.emit('user.join', {
name: name
        });

        $('#messages').prepend(`<p>
<hr />
            Hi ${name}!
</p>`);
    });
});
```

3. Finally, add a server-side event that broadcasts the `user.joined` event on the socket using the following code:

```
io.on('connection', function (socket) {
socket.on('user.join', function (data) {
socket.broadcast.emit('user.joined', data);
    });
});
```

How it works...

The `socket.broadcast.emit()` method sends the message to every socket, except for the socket that the method is called from. Using this method, we can exclude the initiating socket from receiving the event.

Building a multiplayer tic-tac-toe game

We can observe the real power of Socket.IO by using it in a multiplayer game. Although there are many examples of multiplayer games we could implement, tic-tac-toe is one of the more simple games.

The game board is always three tiles long and three tiles tall. The goal is for either user to select any three tiles in a row.

Our final user interface will look something similar to the following image:

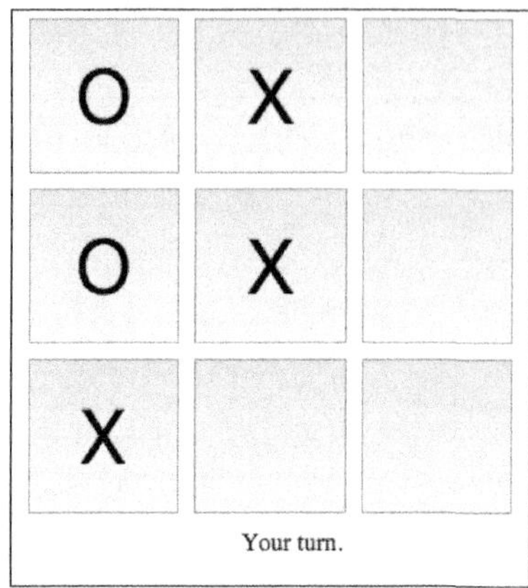

Our game will allow any number of players to join and be paired with another player. The paired players will be able to interact on the board together in real time.

Getting ready

In this recipe, we will use jQuery for the DOM manipulation and event delegation.

How to do it...

To create a real-time multiplayer tic-tac-toe game, follow these instructions:

1. First, create a `server.js` file to handle the server-side portion of our game. Make sure that you create an instantiated Socket.IO connection on your server before you add the following code:

```
var players = {},
      unmatched;

function joinGame (socket) {

    // Add the player to our object of players
    players[socket.id] = {

        // The opponent will either be the socket that is
        // currently unmatched, or it will be null if no
        // players are unmatched
opponent: unmatched,

        // The symbol will become 'O' if the player is
unmatched
```

```
        symbol: 'X',

        // The socket that is associated with this player
        socket: socket
    };

    // Every other player is marked as 'unmatched', which
means
    // there is not another player to pair them with yet.
As soon
    // as the next socket joins, the unmatched player is
paired with
    // the new socket and the unmatched variable is set
back to null
    if (unmatched) {
        players[socket.id].symbol = 'O';
        players[unmatched].opponent = socket.id;
        unmatched = null;

    } else {
        unmatched = socket.id;
    }
}

// Returns the opponent socket
function getOpponent (socket) {
    if (!players[socket.id].opponent) {
        return;
    }

    return players[
        players[socket.id].opponent
    ].socket;
}

io.on('connection', function (socket) {

joinGame(socket);

    // Once the socket has an opponent, we can begin the
game
    if (getOpponent(socket)) {
        socket.emit('game.begin', {
```

```
                symbol: players[socket.id].symbol
            });

            getOpponent(socket).emit('game.begin', {
                symbol: players[getOpponent(socket).id].symbol
            });
        }

        // Listens for a move to be made and emits an event to
    both
        // players after the move is completed
        socket.on('make.move', function (data) {
        if (!getOpponent(socket)) {
            return;
        }

        socket.emit('move.made', data);
        getOpponent(socket).emit('move.made', data);
    });

        // Emit an event to the opponent when the player leaves
        socket.on('disconnect', function () {
            if (getOpponent(socket)) {
                getOpponent(socket).emit('opponent.left');
            }
         });
    });
```

2. Then, create an `index.html` template for a view of our game with the following code:

```
<div class="board">
<button id="a0"></button>
<button id="a1"></button>
<button id="a2"></button>
<button id="b0"></button>
<button id="b1"></button>
<button id="b2"></button>
<button id="c0"></button>
<button id="c1"></button>
<button id="c2"></button>
<div id="messages">Waiting for opponent to join...</div>
</div>
```

3. Now, write the client-side JavaScript to handle the game play, as shown in the following code:

```
VarmyTurn = true, symbol;

function getBoardState () {
varobj = {};

    // We will compose an object of all of the Xs and Ox
    // that are on the board
    $('.board button').each(function () {
        obj[$(this).attr('id')] = $(this).text() || '';
    });

    return obj;
}

function isGameOver () {

    var state = getBoardState(),

        // One of the rows must be equal to either of these
        // value for
        // the game to be over
        matches = ['XXX', 'OOO'],

        // These are all of the possible combinations
        // that would win the game
        rows = [
            state.a0 + state.a1 + state.a2,
            state.b0 + state.b1 + state.b2,
            state.c0 + state.c1 + state.c2,
            state.a0 + state.b1 + state.c2,
            state.a2 + state.b1 + state.c0,
            state.a0 + state.b0 + state.c0,
            state.a1 + state.b1 + state.c1,
            state.a2 + state.b2 + state.c2
        ];

    // Loop over all of the rows and check if any of them
compare
    // to either 'XXX' or 'OOO'
    for (vari = 0; i<rows.length; i++) {
        if (rows[i] === matches[0] || rows[i] ===
matches[1]) {
            return true;
        }
```

```
        }
    }

    function renderTurnMessage () {

        // Disable the board if it is the opponents turn
        if (!myTurn) {
            $('#messages').text('Your opponent\'s turn');
            $('.board button').attr('disabled', true);

        // Enable the board if it is your turn
        } else {
            $('#messages').text('Your turn.');
            $('.board button').removeAttr('disabled');
        }
    }

    function makeMove (e) {
        e.preventDefault();

        // It's not your turn
        if (!myTurn) {
            return;
        }

        // The space is already checked
        if ($(this).text().length) {
            return;
        }

        // Emit the move to the server
        socket.emit('make.move', {
            symbol: symbol,
            position: $(this).attr('id')
        });

    }

    // Event is called when either player makes a move
    socket.on('move.made', function (data) {

        // Render the move
        $('#' + data.position).text(data.symbol);

        // If the symbol is the same as the player's symbol,
        // we can assume it is their turn
```

```
    myTurn = (data.symbol !== symbol);

    // If the game is still going, show who's turn it is
if (!isGameOver()) {
    renderTurnMessage();

    // If the game is over
    } else {

        // Show the message for the loser
       if (myTurn) {
            $('#messages').text('Game over. You lost.');

        // Show the message for the winner
        } else {
            $('#messages').text('Game over. You won!');
        }

        // Disable the board
        $('.board button').attr('disabled', true);
    }
});

// Set up the initial state when the game begins
socket.on('game.begin', function (data) {

    // The server will asign X or O to the player
symbol = data.symbol;

    // Give X the first turn
myTurn = (symbol === 'X');
    renderTurnMessage();
});

// Disable the board if the opponent leaves
socket.on('opponent.left', function () {
    $('#messages').text('Your opponent left the game.');
    $('.board button').attr('disabled', true);
});

$(function () {
    $('.board button').attr('disabled', true);
    $('.board> button').on('click', makeMove);
});
```

4. Then, let's add some CSS to make the board look nice, as shown in the following code:

```
body {
    text-align: center;
}
.board {
    margin: auto;
    width: 350px;
}
.board button {
    height: 100px;
    width: 100px;
    margin: 0px;
    padding: 0px;
    float: left;
    margin-right: 10px;
    margin-bottom: 10px;
    font-size: 3em
}
```

How it works...

Our server is responsible for pairing up sockets as opponents and emitting events to the paired sockets whenever a move is made or the state of the game changes in any way. Most of the actual game logic occurs on the client side, where we keep track of the squares that are selected, who selected them, and who's turn it currently is.

It is important to manage the state of multiplayer games on the server so that all players can use the same state at all times. When the first player makes a move, the state on the server should get updated and the change should then be broadcast to all sockets that are involved in the game.

4
Building a Room with a View

In this chapter, we will cover the following recipes:

- Creating chat channels with namespaces
- Joining rooms
- Leaving rooms
- Listing the rooms that the socket is in
- Creating private rooms
- Setting up a default room

Introduction

Socket.IO uses namespaces to keep separate types of messages from colliding with each other. With namespaces, we can be sure that our applications are listening for the correct events.

We can also define arbitrary rooms that our sockets can join or leave. These rooms restrict someone from receiving messages and send them only to interested parties.

In this chapter, you will also learn how to harness namespaces and rooms to create richer real-time experiences.

Creating chat channels with namespaces

Namespaces are a great way to make sure that our Socket.IO events are not emitted globally to all the sockets that are connected to the server. We can send messages to a namespace. Only the sockets listening to this namespace will receive the event.

Many applications have multiple customers that should never be mixed together. In our URLs, we typically show the use of different domains to keep our customers separate so that `customer1.website.com` has a different result to `customer2.website.com`. In the same way, our Socket.IO sockets can be namespaced to minimize concerns about intermingling data and messaging.

In this recipe, we will set up two separate groups of chat channels. We can post to either group. The message will be restricted to the namespace for that group.

Our interface will be a split page with two separate groups. We can post to either group. The messages will show up after that group, as shown in the following screenshot:

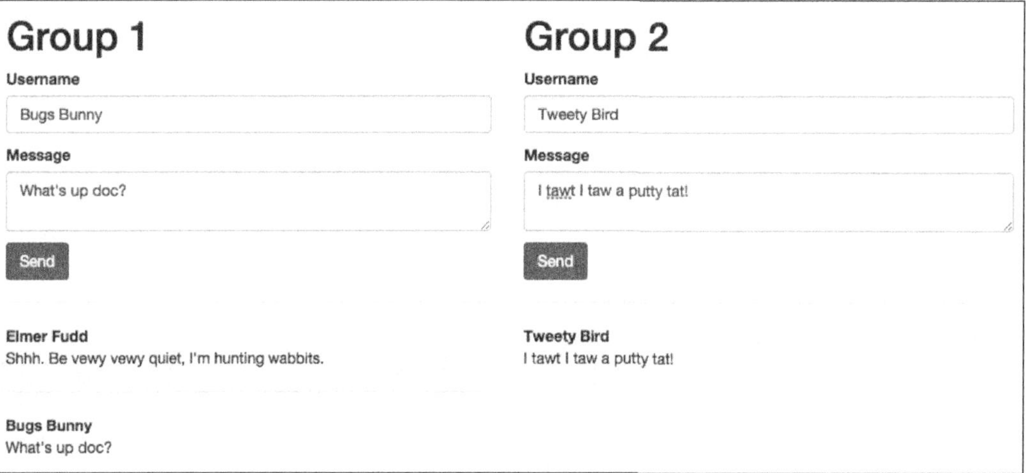

Getting ready

For this recipe, we will use jQuery for the DOM manipulation and Twitter Bootstrap for styling purposes.

How to do it...

To create chat channels with namespaces, follow these instructions:

1. First, add your server-side code. We will create a loop to call a function that will set up our two different namespaces:

```
function createNamespace (i) {
    var group = io.of('/group-' + i);
    group.on('connection', function(socket) {
        socket.on('message.send', function (data) {
        group.emit('message.sent', data);
        });
    });
}

for (var i = 0; i< 2; i++) {
    createNamespace(i);
}
```

2. Now, create your client-side template. Note that most of the template is actually in a `script` tag. The template in this `script` tag will not be executed when the page loads. We will grab it with JavaScript and manipulate it before it is rendered to the DOM:

```
<div class="container">
    <div class="row"></div>
</div>

<script type="text/tpl" id="namespace-group-tpl">
    <div class="col-md-6">
        <h1>Group ${i}</h1>
        <form class="message-form">
            <p>
                <label>Username</label>
                <input class="form-control input-username"
/>
            </p>
            <p>
                <label>Message</label>
                <textarea class="form-control input-
message"></textarea>
            </p>
            <button class="btnbtn-primary"
type="submit">Send</button>
        </form>
        <div class="messages"></div>
    </div>
</script>
```

3. Finally, we will create our client-side JavaScript. Our script will call the `createNamespace()` function twice in a loop to create two unique namespaces and render the interface to display these namespaces, as shown in the following code:

```
functioncreateNamespace (i, template) {
var socket = io(`http://localhost:5000/group-${i}`),
        $el = $(template.replace(/\${i}/g, (i + 1)));

    $('.row').append($el);

    $el.find('.message-form').bind('submit', function (e) {
        e.preventDefault();
        socket.emit('message.send', {
            message: $el.find('.input-message').val(),
            username: $el.find('.input-username').val()
        });
    });

    // Update the users count
    socket.on('message.sent', function (data) {
        $el.find('.messages').prepend(`
            <div>
                <hr />
<div><strong>${data.username}</strong></div>
                <p>${data.message}</p>
            </div>
        `);
    });
}

$(function () {
    var template = $('#namespace-group-tpl').text();

    for (var i= 0; i< 2; i++) {
        createNamespace(i, template);
    }

});
```

How it works...

On the server side of our application, the `io.of()` method was used to create a namespace. It took a string with the name of the namespace as the first argument. The namespace name was important because we also used it on the client side.

On the client side, we just needed to add the namespace to the end of our first argument in the `io()` method. In our example, we instantiated the namespace with the port number as `io.of('http://localhost:5000/my-namespace')`. However, if we were listening on port `80` instead of port `5000`, we could actually just pass the namespace name and not worry about providing the port: `io.of('/my-namespace')`.

Joining rooms

In addition to namespaces, we can also use rooms in Socket.IO to ensure that our messages are only being delivered to the correct sockets.

Although each socket can only have a single namespace, these sockets can belong to multiple rooms. You can think of rooms as channels that a socket subscribes to in order to receive specific types of messages.

For example, if we built a programming application, the user may be interested in JavaScript and Node messages, but not Ruby or C#. With rooms, we can allow users to send messages to specific channels so that only the interested parties will receive it.

As rooms can only be joined if we know the name of the room, it creates a sort of sudo-security. But it is a bit of a hack because if someone can guess the room name and it is exposed to the client to join, they can join any arbitrary room.

In this recipe, we will demonstrate how a user can join a room.

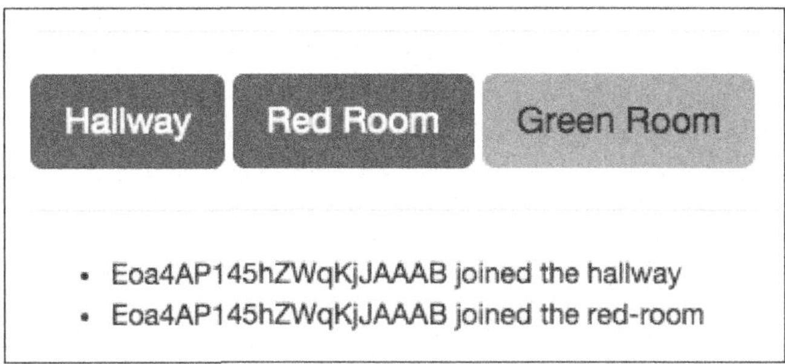

Getting ready

In this recipe, we will use jQuery for some simple DOM manipulation.

How to do it...

To enable the joining of rooms in Socket.IO, follow these steps:

1. First, let's add the server-side room implementation. This includes allowing a socket to join a room with the `socket.join()` method and then emitting a new message to ensure that the socket correctly joined, as shown in the following code:

```
io.on('connection', function (socket) {
    socket.emit('room.joined', socket.id + ' joined the
hallway');
    socket.on('room.join', function (room) {
        socket.join(room);
        io.to(room).emit('room.joined', socket.id + '
joined the ' + room);
    });
});
```

2. Now, add the client-side template with the following code:

```
<button data-id="hallway" class="btn-
primary">Hallway</button>
<button data-id="red-room">Red Room</button>
<button data-id="green-room">Green Room</button>
<ul id="messages"></ul>
```

3. Then, add the client-side JavaScript, as shown in the following code:

```
var socket = io('http://localhost:5000');

socket.on('room.joined', function (message) {
    $('#messages').append(`<li>${message}</li>`);
});

$('button').on('click', function () {
    var id = $(this).data('id');
    if (!$(this).hasClass('btn-primary')) {
        $(this).addClass('btn-primary');
socket.emit('room.join', id);
    }
});
```

How it works...

Socket.IO can emit messages to any arbitrary room name with the `io.on(:room_name).emit()` method. It should be noted that you can emit to a room name whether or not the room already exists beforehand, so there is no need to perform any checking to make sure that the room is available.

When we click on the button in our interface to join one of our rooms, the socket will emit a message to the server asking to join that room. The server side will be responsible for adding the socket to the requested group. We will also emit a message to the newly joined room and announce that the user has indeed joined the room.

Leaving rooms

A socket can not only join a room but also leave any room that it is a member of.

This is important if you're building a real-time application. Here, users may want to disable certain notifications. By leaving a room entirely, the client-side socket will never receive the events that are broadcasted to the room that it has left.

In this recipe, we will expose a single room to the client-side sockets. We will allow the room to be joined or remain separate by simply toggling a checkbox.

The server side will emit a message every two seconds with an ongoing count of how many times the notification has been sent. Therefore, we will be able to turn the notifications on and see the notification numbers logged one after another in a particular order. Then, we can turn it off for a few seconds and finally turn it back on and see the notification number resume after skipping the numbers it would have emitted when it was off.

☐ Get notifications

- This is notification number 8511
- This is notification number 8510
- This is notification number 8509

Getting ready

In this recipe, we will use a little jQuery for the DOM manipulation.

How to do it...

To enable a socket to leave a room, follow these steps:

1. In our server-side code, we will create an event to join the notifications room. We will also create an event that allows the socket to leave the room, as shown in the following code:

```
io.on('connection', function (socket) {
socket.on('notifications.join', function () {
socket.join('notifications');
    });

socket.on('notifications.leave', function () {
socket.leave('notifications');
    });
});


// We will emit a message to every member
// of our room every two seconds with a notification
number.

Var i= 0;

setInterval(function () {
    io.to('notifications').emit('notify', 'This is
notification number ' + i);
    i++;
}, 2000);
```

2. On the client side, we will create a template with a checkbox that allows you to turn the membership of the notifications room on and off. We'll also include a container unordered list to place our messages when they are emitted to us.

```
<div class="container">
    <hr />
    <input type="checkbox" id="toggle" /> Get notifications
    <hr />
    <ul id="messages">
        <!-- Messages will go here -->
    </ul>
</div>
```

3. Finally, we will add some client-side JavaScript to turn our group membership on and off and add messages when we receive them, as shown in the following code:

```
socket.on('notify', function (message) {
    $('#messages').prepend(`<li>${message}</li>`);
});

$(function () {
    $('#toggle').on('click', function () {
        var checked = $(this).is(':checked'),
            action = (checked) ? 'join' : 'leave';

        socket.emit(`notifications.${action}`);
    });
});
```

How it works...

We will emit a message to our notifications room with an interval of two seconds. The portion of our code that will emit the notification doesn't care whether or not any sockets are subscribed to the room that it will emit to. It just blindly emits messages to the room.

We will allow our sockets to join and leave the room by listening for an event from the client.

When our client-side socket is a member of our room, it will receive notifications in the room, but when it is not a member of the room, no notifications will be received.

Listing rooms the socket is in

Socket.IO provides a dynamic list of the rooms that each socket is a member of. We can retrieve this list and use it as needed.

In this recipe, we will create a list of the rooms that our socket is in. The list will be dynamically updated if the socket leaves any of its rooms.

Getting ready

As usual, this recipe will use jQuery for the DOM manipulation and event delegation.

How to do it...

To list the rooms that your socket is in, follow these steps:

1. On the server, we will add our socket to three distinct groups by default. We will add an event listener that will request to list the rooms for us. When this event is sent, we will emit a response message that contains `socket.rooms`, which is an array that Socket.IO builds dynamically as you join and leave rooms. Take a look at the following code:

```
io.on('connection', function (socket) {

    socket.join('room1');
    socket.join('room2');
    socket.join('room3');

    socket.on('list.rooms', function () {
        socket.emit('list.rooms.response', socket.rooms);
    });

    socket.on('leave.room', function (room) {
        socket.leave(room);
    });

});
```

2. Now we will need a simple template to display our room names. We can create this on the client-side, as shown in the following code:

```
<div class="container">
    <h1>My Rooms</h1>
    <ul id="messages"></ul>
</div>
```

3. When the server emits a `list.rooms.response` event, we will need to display it in our template.

```
socket.on('list.rooms.response', function (rooms) {
    $('#messages').html('');
    rooms.forEach(function (room) {
        $('#messages').append(`<li>${room} | <a href="#"
data-id="${room}">leave</a></li>`);
    });
});
```

4. Finally, we will emit the initial event to list our rooms and add a nonClick function to leave any of our rooms with the following code:

```
$(function () {
    socket.emit('list.rooms');
    $('#messages').delegate('a', 'click', function () {
        socket.emit('leave.room', $(this).data('id'));

        // Since we are already listing the rooms initially
with
        // this message, we can do reuse it to kick off the
        // listing response message.
        socket.emit('list.rooms');
    });
});
```

How it works...

The `socket.rooms` variable is an array that contains strings that represents the rooms that our socket is a member of. Whenever we need to send the list of rooms to the client, we can just emit `socket.rooms`. As a result, the client will have a fresh list.

There's more...

You may have seen that there is a room with a random name. It will look something similar to `GGYnSGkjSLxhfCnVAAAB`. This is the default room that the socket is associated with. Each socket has its own room when it is connected. We will explore this in more details in the *Setting up a default room* recipe later in this chapter.

Creating private rooms

It can often be useful to provide privacy for certain rooms. This allows you to send messages to a small group of sockets without worrying about the messages being received by sockets that should not be allowed to see them.

Although Socket.IO doesn't have any inbuilt way to consider a room private or public, we can add some logic around joining a room so that only sockets that validate against a password check are allowed to be members of the room.

In this recipe, we will create a simple login page. Sockets can log in with the static password: `pass123`, but we could easily make it use a dynamic password that comes from our database or an environmental variable. When the socket joins a group, it will be able to see all the messages that are emitted to this group as expected.

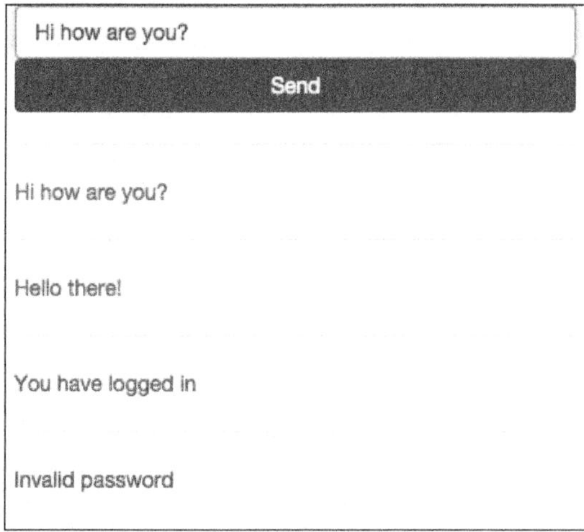

Getting ready

For this recipe, we will use jQuery for the DOM manipulation.

We will also make use of the MD5 Node module to hash our password. Although it may seem silly to hash a password that is hardcoded like this, typically, our password would not be included in the code at all. As best practice, it should either be in a database or an environmental variable. We can install the MD5 package by entering `npm install md5 -save` in the terminal.

How to do it...

To create a private room, follow these steps:

1. First, add your server-side code. This will perform some validation before the socket joins a room to ensure that they have entered the correct password, as shown in the following code:

```
// Include the md5 module
var md5 = require('MD5');

// This is the hashed password to join the private group
```

```
// It is the md5 hash of "pass123"


io.on('connection', function (socket) {

    socket.on('join.group', function (data) {

        // Return and emit a message if the passwords don't
match
        if (md5(data.password) !== privatePassword) {
            returnsocket.emit('message.posted', {
                type: 'danger',
                message: 'Invalid password'
            });
        }

        // Join the group
        socket.join('secret group');
        socket.emit('join.group.success');
    });

    // Post a message to the secret group
    socket.on('message.post', function (data) {
        io.to('secret group').emit('message.posted', {
            type: 'muted',
            message: data.message
        });
    });

});

io.on('connection', function (socket) {

socket.on('join.group', function (data) {

        // Return and emit a message if the passwords don't
match
    if (md5(data.password) !== privatePassword) {
        return socket.emit('message.posted', {
            type: 'danger',
            message: 'Invalid password'
```

```
            });
        }

          // Join the group
        socket.join('secret group');
            socket.emit('join.group.success');
        });

        // Post a message to the secret group
        socket.on('message.post', function (data) {
            io.to('secret group').emit('message.posted', {
                type: 'muted',
                message: data.message
            });
        });
```

2. Then, create the client-side template. This will include a form to log in and a form to post messages. The messages form will only be displayed after the socket joins the room. Take a look at the following code:

```
<div class="container">

<!-- Login Form -->
<form id="login">
    <div class="row">
        <div class="col-md-9">
            <input class="form-control"
placeholder="Password" type="password" />
        </div>
        <div class="col-md-3">
            <button class="btnbtn-primary form-
control">Login</button>
        </div>
    </div>
</form>

<!-- Message -->
<form id="message" style="display: none">
    <div class="row">
        <div class="col-md-9">
            <input class="form-control"
placeholder="Message" />
        </div>
        <div class="col-md-3">
```

```
            <button class="btnbtn-primary form-
control">Send</button>
        </div>
    </div>
</form>

<div id="messages"></div>
</div>
```

3. Now, let's add our client-side logic. This will mainly just listen for events that are triggered when the login form is submitted or a message is sent, as shown in the following code:

```
// Render messages from the server
function renderMessage (data) {
    $('#messages').prepend(`<div class="text-${data.type}">
        <hr />
        <p>${data.message}</p>
    </div>`);
}

socket.on('message.posted', renderMessage);

// Toggle the messages and login form when the socket logs
in
socket.on('join.group.success', function () {
    $('#message').show();
    $('#login').hide();
    renderMessage({
        type: 'success',
        message: 'You have logged in'
    });
});

$(function () {

    // Attempt to log in
    $('#login').on('submit', function (e) {
        e.preventDefault();
        var password = $(this).find('input').val();
        socket.emit('join.group', {
            password: password
        });
    });

    // Send a message
```

```
        $('#message').on('submit', function (e) {
            e.preventDefault();
            var message = $(this).find('input').val();
            socket.emit('message.post', {
                message: message
            });
        });
    });
```

How it works...

By returning before the socket joins a room, we will be able to keep the code underneath the return from executing if the password entered by the user doesn't match the password we expect.

As we will hash our password, we will need to hash the value that the socket sends us so that we can compare the two.

Setting up a default room

In Socket.IO, every socket that makes a connection is assigned a default room to emit messages. This default room could be used for a wide variety of purposes.

A practical use of the default room is to store friends or followers of the socket. When another socket joins the default room of a socket, we can assume that the socket is interested in receiving updates from the room that it has joined.

Other sockets are able to join the default room of any other socket. It isn't safe to assume that the default room of a socket only has one member unless the server-side architecture is set up in this way.

In this recipe, we will let our socket emit messages to the default room of any other connected socket. We will build a drop-down list that displays all of our sockets. Also, the client can select the socket that it wants to emit messages to.

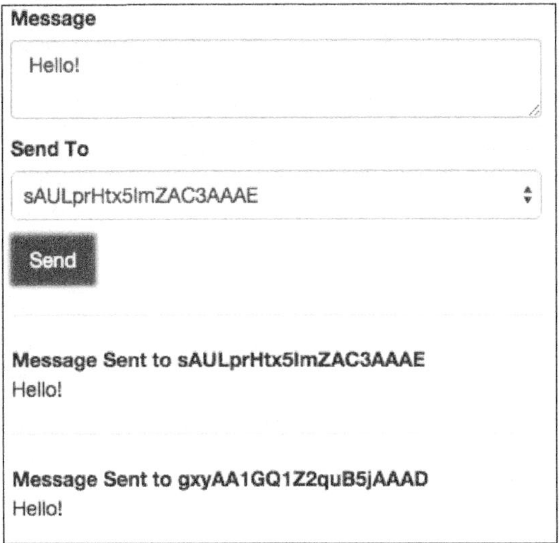

Getting ready

For this recipe, we will use jQuery for the event delegation and DOM manipulation.

How to do it...

To emit messages to the default room for any connected socket, follow these steps:

1. In our server-side code, we will emit a `socket.joined` message with the socket ID and the default room string. We will also create a listener to send a message to any room ID, in which it is passed, as shown in the following code:

```
io.on('connection', function (socket) {

    // When a socket connects, the default room will be
    // the first item in the socket.rooms array
    socket.broadcast.emit('socket.joined', {
        userId: socket.id,
        room: socket.rooms[0]
    });

    socket.on('message.send', function (data) {
        socket.broadcast.to(data.id).emit('message.sent', {
            id: socket.id,
```

```
                message: data.message
            });
        });
    });
```

2. Now, using the following code, let's create a client-side template with a form to submit messages to any selected room:

```
<div class="container">
    <form id="message-form">
    <p>
        <label>Message</label>
        <textarea id="message" class="form-control input-
message"></textarea>
    </p>
    <p>
        <label>Send To</label>
        <select id="send-to" class="form-control">
            <!-- This will be populated by JavaScript -->
        </select>
    </p>
    <button class="btnbtn-primary"
type="submit">Send</button>
    </form>
    <div id="messages"></div>
</div>
```

3. Finally, we will write our client-side JavaScript. This will send messages to the server and listen to messages from the server, which we will display in the UI of our application. Take a look at the following code:

```
function messageSent (data) {
    $('#messages').prepend(`
<p>
    <hr />
    <strong>${data.id}</strong><br />
    ${data.message}
</p>
    `);
}

socket.on('socket.joined', function (user) {
```

```
        $('#send-to').append(`<option>${user.userId}</option>`);
    });

    socket.on('message.sent', messageSent);

    $(function () {
        $('#message-form').on('submit', function (e) {
            e.preventDefault();
            messageSent({
                id: 'Message Sent to ' +  $('#send-to').val(),
                message: $('#message').val()
            });

        socket.emit('message.send', {
            id: $('#send-to').val(),
            message: $('#message').val()
        });
    });
    });
```

How it works...

When each of our sockets created a connection, they were assigned a unique room with an unguessable random name. We could use this to emit messages to the socket and any other sockets that may join it.

We sent messages to our new room using the `socket.broadcast.to()` method. This method took the room name as its only argument and then exposed the `emit()` method to broadcast messages. When we sent messages using the room specified in `socket.broadcast.to()`, they were only delivered to sockets that were members of the newly created room.

5

Securing Your Data

In this chapter, we will cover the following recipes:

- Implementing basic authentication
- Performing token-based authentication
- Handling server-side validation
- Locking down the HTTP referrer
- Using secure WebSockets

Introduction

Although the WebSocket protocol provides several opportunities for more direct communication between the client and the server, people often wonder if Socket.IO is actually as secure as something similar to the HTTP protocol. The answer to this question is that it depends entirely on how you implement it. WebSockets can be easily controlled to prevent malicious or accidental security holes, but with any API interface, your security is only as tight as your weakest link.

In this chapter, we will explore several topics related to security in Socket.IO applications. From authentication and validation to how to use the `wss://` protocol for secure WebSockets, these topics will cover the entire gamut.

Implementing basic authentication

Most applications need a way to authenticate users. In this recipe, we will create a simple form to create and authenticate users. We will keep our authenticated users in the session so that we can maintain our authenticated state even when the page is refreshed. In order to get our users, we will pass a random token to the socket, once it authenticates, that it can use to retrieve the authenticated profile.

Getting ready

For this recipe, we will use MongoDB to persist our users. We will also use the the `md5 npm` module to hash our passwords before we save them to the database.

How to do it...

To implement basic authentication, follow these steps:

1. First, we will need to create our server. The server will require several additional modules that we will build next. Use the following code:

```
var express = require('express'),
    app = express(),
    http = require('http'),
    socketIO = require('socket.io'),
    server, io;

app.get('/', function (req, res) {
     res.sendFile(__dirname + '/index.html');
});

server = http.Server(app);
server.listen(5000);

io = socketIO(server);

var getUser = require('./lib/getUser'),
       loginUser = require('./lib/loginUser'),
       createUser = require('./lib/createUser'),
       authenticateUser = require('./lib/authenticateUser');

global.userSessions = {};

io.on('connection', function (socket) {
```

```
    // Get the authenticated user
     socket.on('user.get', function (token) {
          getUser(socket, token);
    });

     // Create a new user
     socket.on('user.create', function (data) {
          console.log('user.create');
          createUser(socket, data);
    });

     // Login
     socket.on('user.login', function (data) {
          authenticateUser(socket, data);
    });

     // Log the authenticated user out
     socket.on('user.logout', function (token) {
          delete userSessions[token];
    });
});
```

2. Next, we will create a `getUser` module in our `/lib` folder that will be responsible for retrieving authenticated users that match the token we pass to it:

```
// Get a user who matches the token
module.exports = function getUser (socket, token) {

  // Emit an error if the token doesn't exist
if (!userSessions[token]) {
     return socket.emit('user.get.error', {
          message: 'This user is not authenticated'
      });
  }

     // Emit a message with the profile and token
     // if the token does exist
     return socket.emit('user.get.success', {
          profile: userSessions[token],
          token: token
    });

};
```

3. Now, we will need to create a `loginUser` module in the same directory. This will be responsible for setting a user in the session if it authenticates. Note that we will use the crypto module to encode our token, as shown in the following code:

```
var crypto = require('crypto'),
    getUser = require('./getUser');

// Logs in a user
module.exports = function loginUser (socket, user) {

    // Create a token with crypto
    var token = crypto.randomBytes(64).toString('base64');

    // Save the user session
    userSessions[token] = user;

   // Get the user belonging to the token and emit it
    return getUser(socket, token);
};
```

4. We won't be able to log a user in unless we create a user first, so we will add a `createUser` module. This will use the MD5 module to hash our password. You can install this by running `npm install MD5 -save` in your terminal with the following code:

```
var md5 = require('md5'),
     User = require('./userModel'),
     loginUser = require('./loginUser');

// Creates a new user
module.exports = function createUser (socket, data) {

    // Hash the password
    data.password = md5(data.password);

    // Create a new user in MongoDB
    var user = new User(data);

    // Save the MongoDB Model
    user.save().then(function (data) {
        return loginUser(socket, data);
  });

};
```

5. Next, we will need to add an `authenticateUser` module to help us log our users in. This will attempt to find a user with a username and password that match the combination that the user enters. If a user is found, they will be logged in. If no user is found, we will emit an error message. Note that we will hash the password before we attempt to find a matching user. The password in the database is hashed, so we will want to match this, as shown in the following code:

```
var md5 = require('md5'),
      User = require('./userModel'),
      loginUser = require('./loginUser');

// Authenticates a user and logs them in
module.exports = function authenticateUser (socket, data) {

     // Hash the password
     data.password = md5(data.password);

     User.findOne(data, null, function (err, data) {

          // If the username and password are correct, log
the user in
          if (data) {
               return loginUser(socket, data);

          // If the username or password are incorrect,
emit an error
          } else {
               return socket.emit('user.login.error', err
|| {
                    message: 'Invalid email or password.'
          });
      }
  });

};
```

6. Now, let's create our `userModel`. This will be a MongoDB model that we can interact with to add and retrieve users, as shown in the following code:

```
var mongoose = require('mongoose');

var db =
mongoose.connect('mongodb://localhost/basicauthapp');

var userSchema = db.Schema({
     firstname: String,
```

```
        lastname: String,
        password: { type: String, select: false },
        email: String
});

module.exports = db.model('User', userSchema);
```

7. Now for the client-side. We will need a container for our views to get rendered to:

```
<div class="container" id="main-container"></div>
```

8. For our client-side JavaScript, the following code mainly just listens for messages from Socket.IO and performs some basic routing when the hashtag changes:

```
function renderTemplate (tpl) {
        document.getElementById('main-container').innerHTML =
tpl;
}

function userLoggedIn (data) {
        localStorage.token = data.token;
        renderTemplate(getProfileTemplate(data.profile));
        profileController(data);
}

functiongetRoute () {

        if (document.location.hash === '#/create-account') {
            renderTemplate(getCreateAccountTemplate());
            createAccountController();
            return;
        }

        renderTemplate(getLoginTemplate());
        loginController();
}

function showError (data) {
        alert(data.message)
}

(function () {
        socket.on('user.create.error', showError);
        socket.on('user.get.success', userLoggedIn);
        socket.on('user.login.error', showError);
```

```
    window.addEventListener('hashchange', getRoute);

    getRoute();

     // If we have a token, send it to the server to
authenticate
    if (localStorage.token) {
        socket.emit('user.get', localStorage.token);
    }
}());
```

9. We will also need some logic to render our **Create Account** form and emit an event to Socket.IO when the form is submitted. This will look something like this when the view is active:

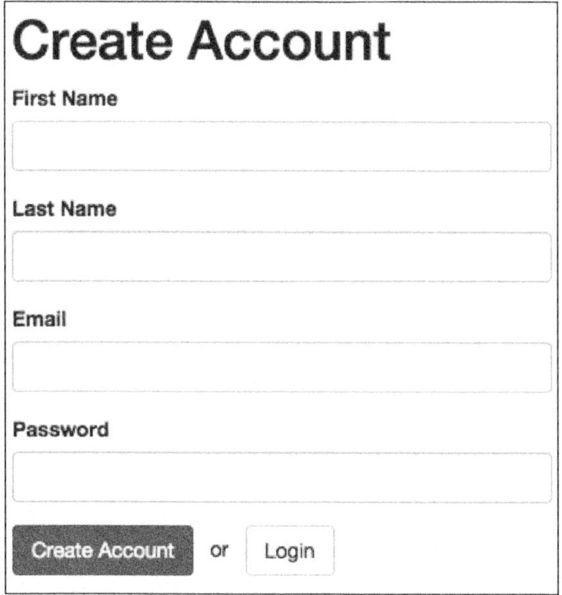

Use the following code to implement this:

```
function getCreateAccountTemplate () {
return `
<form id="create-account-form">

    <h1>Create Account</h1>

    <div class="form-group">
```

```
            <label>First Name</label>
            <input id="firstname" class="form-control" />
        </div>

        <div class="form-group">
            <label>Last Name</label>
            <input id="lastname" class="form-control" />
        </div>

        <div class="form-group">
            <label>Email</label>
            <input id="email" type="email" class="form-
control" />
        </div>

        <div class="form-group">
            <label>Password</label>
            <input id="password" type="password" class="form-
control" />
        </div>

        <div class="form-group">
            <button class="btn btn-primary">Create
Account</button>
              or  
            <a href="#/" class="btn btn-default">Login</a>
        </div>

    <div id="messages"></div>

    </form>
        `;
    }

    function createAccountController () {
        document.getElementById('create-account-form')
            .addEventListener('submit', function (e) {
                e.preventDefault();

                var user = {
                    email: document.getElementById('email').value,
                    password: document.getElementById('password').
value,
                    firstname: document.
getElementById('firstname').value,
```

```
                    lastname: document.getElementById('lastname').
value
                };

                socket.emit('user.create', user);
        });
}
```

10. We will also create a template to display our login form, as shown in the following screenshot:

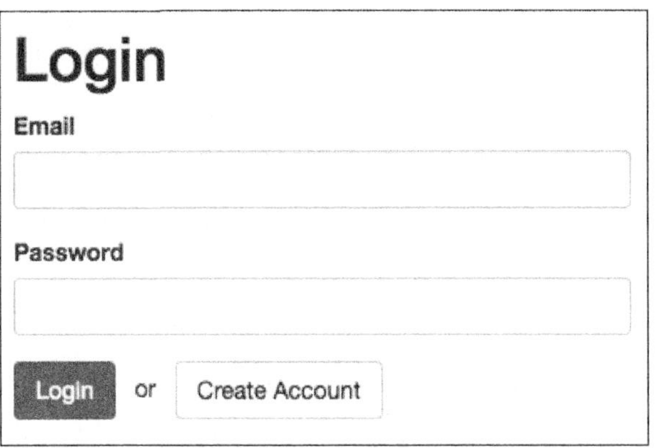

Use the following code to do this:

```
function getLoginTemplate () {
return `
<form id="login-form">

     <h1>Login</h1>

     <div class="form-group">
          <label>Email</label>
          <input id="email" type="email" class="form-
control" />
     </div>

     <div class="form-group">
          <label>Password</label>
          <input id="password" type="password" class="form-
control" />
     </div>
```

```
        <div class="form-group">
            <button class="btn btn-primary">Login</button>
              or  
            <a href="#/create-account" class="btnbtn-
default">Create Account</a>
        </div>

        <div id="messages"></div>

</form>
    `;
}

function loginController () {
        document.getElementById('login-form')
            .addEventListener('submit', function (e) {
                e.preventDefault();

                var user = {
                    email:
document.getElementById('email').value,
                    password:
document.getElementById('password').value
                };

                socket.emit('user.login', user);
        });
}
```

11. Finally, we will require a template for when the user logs in. We will take an argument to the template function so that we can render some data to it:

Use the following code to do this:

```
function getProfileTemplate (profile) {
return `
```

```
<div>
     <h1>Hello ${profile.firstname}!</h1>
     <p>You are logged in.</p>

     <div class="form-group">
          <button id="logout" class="btn btn-
primary">Logout</button>
     </div>
</div>
    `;
}

function profileController () {
     document.getElementById('logout')
          .addEventListener('click', function (e) {
               e.preventDefault();
               socket.emit('user.logout');
               delete localStorage.token;
               getRoute();
        });
}
```

How it works...

After our user was authenticated, we added them to the session by appending them to an object of users with a token as our key. We also emitted the token back to the client side, where we stored it in `localStorage`. Using this same token, we will be able to prove that we are the authenticated user that we claim to be, so our session will be maintained.

Performing token-based authentication

Now that we are able to perform basic authentication with Socket.IO, let's take a look at a token-based approach that handles authentication more securely, such as JSON Web Tokens, or JWT.

JSON Web Tokens are an URL-safe means of representing claims to be transferred between two parties. The claims in a JSON Web Token are encoded as a JSON object that is digitally signed using JSON Web Signature. With this approach, we can securely send a salted web token to the client to use on subsequent requests.

Getting ready

For this recipe, we will use the `jsonwebtokennpm` package to create secure JSON Web Tokens. The package can be installed by running `npm install jsonwebtoken -save` in your terminal.

How to do it...

To perform token-based authentication, follow these steps:

1. First, let's create our server and expose the events of Socket.IO to authenticate and receive a JSON Web Token. In this example, we will hardcode a profile to be associated with the JWT, but you would typically retrieve a record from your database to represent the authenticated user. Use the following code:

```
var express = require('express'),
       app = express(),
       http = require('http'),
       socketIO = require('socket.io'),
       jwt = require('jsonwebtoken'),
       server, io;

app.get('/', function (req, res) {
     res.sendFile(__dirname + '/index.html');
});

server = http.Server(app);
server.listen(5000);

io = socketIO(server);

io.on('connection', function (socket) {

     // Our JWT secret
     var jwtSecret = 'my b1g $3CR3T';

     // Verifies our JWT token and emits a profile if it
checks out
     function getProfile (data) {
          jwt.verify(data.token, jwtSecret, function(err,
decoded) {

          // Send an error message
          if (err) {
```

```
                return socket.emit('profile.error', err);
            }

            // Send a success message
            socket.emit('profile.success', decoded);
        });
    }

    // Get the profile
    socket.on('profile', getProfile);

    // Log the user in
    socket.on('login', function () {

        var profile = {
            firstName: 'Peter',
            lastName: 'Parker',
            email: 'peterparker@spiderman.com',
            id: 12
        };

        var token = jwt.sign(profile, jwtSecret, {
            expiresInMinutes: 60
        });

        socket.emit('login.success', {
            token: token
        });

        getProfile({
            token: token
        });
    });
});
```

2. On the client side, we will create methods for logging in and logging out of our application. The client will listen for a `login.success` response from the server. When it receives the login success message, it will save the JWT in `localStorage` to authenticate future requests. Use the following code:

```
function renderTemplate (template, data) {
    document.getElementById('main-container').innerHTML =
templates[template](data);
}
```

```
function renderLoggedOut () {
     renderTemplate('loggedOut');

document.getElementById('login').addEventListener('click',
function (e) {
     socket.emit('login');
  });
}

function renderLoggedIn (data) {
     renderTemplate('loggedIn', data);

document.getElementById('logout').addEventListener('click',
function (e) {
           delete localStorage.jwtToken;
           renderLoggedOut();
     });
}

var templates = {
     loggedOut: function () {
          return `
               <div>
                    <h1>You are not logged in.</h1>
                    <button id="login">Login</button>
               </div>`;
             },

     loggedIn: function (data) {
          return `
               <div>
                    <h1>You are logged in as
${data.firstName} ${data.lastName}.</h1>
                    <button id="logout">Logout</button>
          </div>`;
     }
};

socket.on('profile.success', function (data) {
     renderLoggedIn(data);
});
```

```
socket.on('profile.error', function (err) {
    renderLoggedOut();
});

socket.on('login.success', function (data) {
    localStorage.jwtToken = data.token;
});

if (localStorage.jwtToken) {
    socket.emit('profile', {
        token: localStorage.jwtToken
    });

} else {
    renderLoggedOut();
}
```

How it works...

JSON Web Tokens are a secure means of representing an authenticated session because they are signed with a secret passphrase along with the profile. The token looks similar to a long string of random characters, but the server side will be able to verify the token and decode it as needed.

Handling server-side validation

When we write data to a database, it is important to perform validation on the server side to ensure that the data is in the type and format that we expect it to be in. In this recipe, we will demonstrate how we can emit data to the server and emit messages back if there is a success or an error.

Getting ready

We will use promises to handle success and error states. Depending on your version of Node, you may need to install the promise module with `npm install promise -save`. Promises are a feature of ES6, so they will eventually be native in Node.

How to do it...

To handle validation on the server side, follow these steps:

1. First, we will create a method for performing some validation on the server side. Typically, your validation would take place in your ORM, but we will perform it in plain JavaScript here to exhibit the concept. We will resolve a promise if the data is valid and reject the promise if it is invalid. Use the following code:

```
function validatePerson (person) {
     return new Promise (function (resolve, reject) {
          if (!person.firstname.length) {
               return reject({
                    firstname: 'Please provide a first
name.'
               });
          }

          if (!person.lastname.length) {
               return reject({
                    lastname: 'Please provide a last name.'
               });
          }

          if (person.firstname === person.lastname) {
               return reject({
                    lastname: 'Why is your last name the
same your first name? That seems unlikely...'
               });
          }

         // We aren't really saving anything here, but we
can still pretend ;)
         return resolve(person);
  });
}
```

2. Now, we will call our `validatePerson()` method any time the client emits an event to save a person by using the following code. If the data is valid, we can safely save the data and emit an event and announce that the data was saved. A good way to keep track of your success and error messages is to postfix `.success` or `.error` onto the end of the original message name when you create the new message from the server. In this way, your client will always know to listen for the correct message name, and you won't have to spend as much time trying to think of clever message names. You can always expect that, when you save data, the server will reply with a success or error when it is done.

```
io.on('connection', function (socket) {
     socket.on('person.save', function (person) {
          validatePerson(person).then(function (data) {
          socket.emit('person.save.success', data);

          }).catch(function (data) {
               socket.emit('person.save.error', data);
          });
     });
});
```

3. Now, on the client-side, we will need a template to render our form:

```
<div class="container">
     <form id="personform">

               <div class="form-group">
                    <label for="firstname">First
Name</label>
                    <input name="firstname" id="firstname"
class="form-control" />
                    <small class="text-danger"
id="firstname-error"></small>
               </div>

               <div class="form-group">
                    <label for="lastname">Last Name</label>
                    <input name="lastname" id="lastname"
class="form-control" />
                    <small class="text-danger"
id="lastname-error"></small>
               </div>

               <div class="form-group">
                    <button class="btn btn-
primary">Save</button>
               </div>

     </form>
</div>
```

4. Finally, we will add some client-side JavaScript to send data to the server and update the view with messages when it receives a response from the server, as shown in the following code:

```
socket.on('person.save.success', function (data) {
     console.log('success', data);
```

```
        alert(`${data.firstname} ${data.lastname} was
successfully saved`);
    });

    socket.on('person.save.error', function (data) {
        for (vari in data) {
            if (data.hasOwnProperty(i)) {
                document.getElementById(i + '-
error').innerHTML = data[i];
            }
        }
    });

    document.getElementById('personform').addEventListener('sub
mit', function (e) {
        e.preventDefault();
        var person = {
            firstname: document.getElementById('firstname').value,
            lastname: document.getElementById('lastname').value
        };

        for (vari in person) {
            document.getElementById(i + '-error').innerHTML =
'';
        }

        socket.emit('person.save', person);
    });
```

How it works...

The key to good server-side validation with Socket.IO is to always respond with either a success or error message for every request to submit a form. Socket.IO doesn't have a callback as an Ajax call would, so it is important to listen for these events on the client side so that the update can be updated as needed.

Locking down the HTTP referrer

Socket.IO is really good at getting around cross-domain issues when you create a request from a client in a different domain than the domain your server lives on. You can easily include the Socket.IO script from a different domain on your page. It will work just as you may expect it to.

There are some instances where you may not want your Socket.IO events to be available to every other domain. Not to worry! We can easily whitelist only the http referrers that we want so that some domains will be allowed to connect and other domains won't.

How to do it...

To lock down the HTTP referrer and only allow events to whitelisted domains, follow these steps:

1. Create two different servers that can connect to your Socket.IO instance. We will let one server listen on port `5000`, and let the second server listen on port `5001`:

   ```
   var express = require('express'),
          app = express(),
          http = require('http'),
          socketIO = require('socket.io'),
          server, server2, io;

   app.get('/', function (req, res) {
        res.sendFile(__dirname + '/index.html');
   });

   server = http.Server(app);
   server.listen(5000);

   server2 = http.Server(app);
   server2.listen(5001);

   io = socketIO(server);
   ```

2. When the connection is established, check the referrer in the headers. If it is a referrer we want to give access to, we can let our connection do its work and build up events as normal. If a blacklisted referrer, such as the one on port `5001` that we created, attempts a connection, we can politely decline, and perhaps throw an error message back to the client:

   ```
   io.on('connection', function (socket) {
        switch (socket.request.headers.referer) {
   ```

```
            case 'http://localhost:5000/':
                socket.emit('permission.message', 'Okay,
you\'re cool.');
            break;
            default:
                return socket.emit('permission.message',
'Who invited you to this party?');
            break;
        }
});
```

3. On the client-side, we can listen to the response from the server and react as appropriate:

```
<h1></h1>
<script src="http://localhost:5000/socket.io/socket.io.js"></
script
>
<script type="text/javascript">
var socket = io.connect(5000);
socket.on('permission.message', function (data) {
    document.querySelector('h1').innerHTML = data;
});
</script>
```

How it works...

The referrer is always available in the `socket.request.headers` object of every socket, so we were able to inspect it there to see if it was a trusted source.

In our case, we are using a switch statement to whitelist our domain on port `5000`, but we could really use any mechanism at our disposal to do the job. For example, if we need to dynamically whitelist domains, we might store a list of them in our database and search for it when the connection is established.

Using secure WebSockets

WebSocket communications can either take place over the `ws://` protocol or the `wss://` protocol. They can be thought of in similar terms to the HTTP and HTTPS protocols in that one is secure and one isn't. Secure WebSockets are encrypted by the transport layer, so they are safer to use when handling sensitive data. The main feature of HTTPS (and wss) is that socket is encrypted from client to server, so if we're in the same network and we try to sniff the content, we won't see anything legible.

If your application uses the `HTTPS` protocol, you will also need to use the `wss` protocol for your WebSockets. Many browsers do not allow un-secure content when they use HTTPS.

In this recipe, we will learn how to force our Socket.IO communications to happen over the `wss://` protocol for an extra layer of encryption.

Getting ready

In this recipe, we will need to create a self-signing certificate so that we can serve our app locally over the HTTPS protocol. For that, we will need a npm package called **Pem**. Pem allows us to create a self-signed certificate that we can provide to our server. Of course, in a real production environment, we would want a true SSL certificate instead of a self-signed one. To install Pem, simply call `npm install pem -save`.

Since our certificate is self-signed, you will probably see something like this when you go to your secure server:

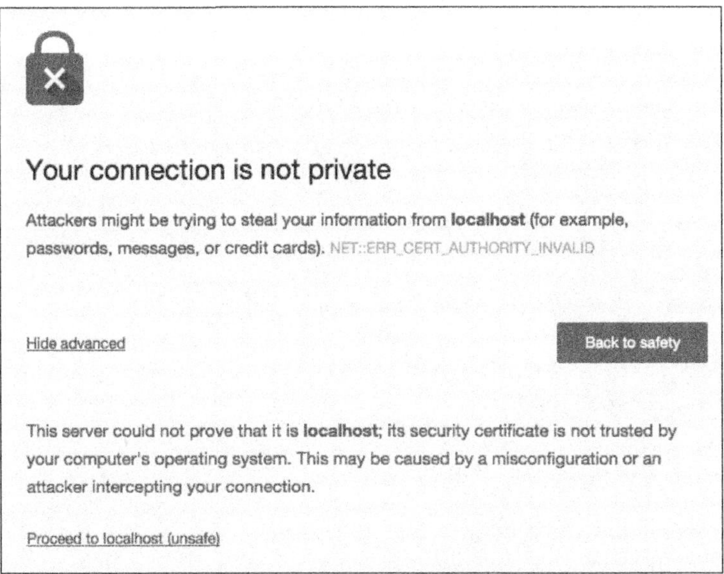

In production, when you purchase a SSL certificate, the warning in your browser will go away. For now, just take a chance by clicking the **Proceed to localhost** link. You'll see your application load using the HTTPS protocol.

How to do it...

To use the secure `wss://` protocol, follow these steps:

1. First, create a secure server using the built-in Node HTTPS package. We can create a self-signed certificate with the `pem` package so that we can serve our application over HTTPS instead of HTTP:

```
var https = require('https'),
       pem = require('pem'),
       express = require('express'),
       app = express(),
       socketIO = require('socket.io');

// Create a self-signed certificate with pem
pem.createCertificate({
    days: 1,
    selfSigned: true
}, function (err, keys) {

app.get('/', function(req, res){
    res.sendFile(__dirname + '/index.html');
});

  // Create an https server with the certificate and key
from pem
var server = https.createServer({
    key: keys.serviceKey,
    cert: keys.certificate
}, app).listen(5000);

var io = socketIO(server);

io.on('connection', function (socket) {
    var protocol = 'ws://';

      // Check the handshake to determine if it was secure
or not
    if (socket.handshake.secure) {
        protocol = 'wss://';
    }
```

```
    socket.emit('hello.client', {
        message: 'This is a message from the server. It was
sent using the ' + protocol + ' protocol'
    });
});
```

2. In your client-side JavaScript, specify `secure: true` when you initialize your WebSocket. This will force the WebSocket connection to be secure. If this is not set, Socket.IO will determine whether or not to use secure WebSockets based on the protocol of your app:

```
<script src="//localhost:5000/socket.io/socket.io.js"
type="text/javascript"></script>
<script type="text/javascript"></>
var socket = io('//localhost:5000', {
     secure: true
});

socket.on('hello.client', function (data) {
    console.log(data);
});
</script>
```

3. Now start your server and go to `https://localhost:5000`. Proceed to the page and you should see a message in your browser developer tools that says **This is a message from the server. It was sent using the wss:// protocol**. We should note that opening servers in non-standard ports can cause problems with users behind firewalls, which only allow traffic to ports `80` and `443`. I would advise using port 80 whenever possible. If you are unable to use either of the standard ports, you may want to do some further reading on reverse proxies to help bypass this problem.

How it works...

The protocol of our WebSocket is actually set automatically based on the protocol of the page that it sits on. This means that a page that is served over the HTTP protocol will send WebSocket communications over `ws://` by default, and a page that is served over HTTPS will default to using the `wss://` protocol.

However, by setting the **Secure** option to **true**, we told the WebSocket to always serve over `wss://` no matter what.

6

Performing a Load Balancing Act

In this chapter, we will cover the following recipes:

- Performing load balancing with the Nginx server
- Using the Node.js cluster
- Using Redis to pass events between nodes
- Using Memcached to manage multiple nodes
- Using RabbitMQ to message events across nodes

Introduction

A single node server can typically handle several thousand simultaneous connections. However, as the audience of an application grows, it is important to make sure that the application is scalable. On the server side, this means that we may want to distribute our applications across multiple threads or node instances.

The issue with distributing your application across nodes is that when we emit a message, it will only be received by one of the distributed servers. Sockets that are not connected to the same server as the one that receives the message will not be able to receive it without some additional handling. Luckily, there are some great ways to pass session data between servers with a caching system, such as Redis, Memcache, or RabbitMQ. By using adapters for one of these distributed caching mechanisms, we can easily scale our servers without compromising our Socket.IO connections.

Performing load balancing with the Nginx server

Nginx is a free, open source, high-performance HTTP server, and reversed proxy. Unlike traditional servers, Nginx doesn't rely on threads to handle requests. Instead, it uses a much more scalable asynchronous architecture. This architecture uses small and predictable amounts of memory under load.

We can use Nginx to load-balance our node servers and, if it is configured correctly, we won't have to worry about requests being lost between the original handshake and the callback when events are received.

Getting ready

Before we can do effective load balancing with the Nginx server, we will need to install it. Nginx can be installed with Homebrew with the following code:

```
brew install nginx
```

Once Nginx is installed, you can start it by running the following code:

```
sudo nginx
```

You can also stop it by running the following code:

```
sudo nginx -s stop
```

How to do it...

To load-balance a Socket.IO app using Nginx, follow these steps:

1. Open your `Nginxconfig` file. This will most likely be located at `/usr/local/etc/nginx/nginx.conf`.
2. Find the HTTP section of the `nginx.conf` file and add your list of upstream nodes, as shown in the following code:

```
upstream io_nodes {
  ip_hash;
  server 127.0.0.1:5000;
  server 127.0.0.1:5001;
  server 127.0.0.1:5002;
  server 127.0.0.1:5003;
}
```

3. On the server or location, configure your proxy to pass all the headers from the original request, as shown in the following code:

```
location / {
    proxy_set_header Upgrade $http_upgrade;
    proxy_set_header Connection "upgrade";
    proxy_set_header X-Forwarded-For
$proxy_add_x_forwarded_for;
    proxy_set_header Host $host;
    proxy_http_version 1.1;
    proxy_pass http://io_nodes;
}
```

4. Start your Nginx server by using `sudonginx`. By default, your server will listen on port `8080`. You can switch it to a different port if you need to in the `nginx.conf` file.

How it works...

The Nginx server will proxy through to your node server or servers. It will dynamically decide which server needs to be hit by looking at `worker_processes`, and `worker_connections`, which is inside the events object as you can see here:

```
events {
    worker_connections  1024;
}
```

The `worker_processes` indicates the number of workers that Nginx should use. By default, it is set to `1`, so it should be bumped to allow multiple workers. You can optimize both of these as needed.

Using the Node.js cluster

Node.js comes with a cluster package that can be used to run Node on multiple threads, as opposed to the single thread that it runs on normally. The child processes that cluster creates will all be able to run on the same port, which means that you can effectively load-balance without running your server on multiple ports.

Unfortunately, there is some boilerplate needed to determine the number of CPUs available to run Node processes and fork the original node. For this, we can use a module called sticky session. This is a load balancer that automatically spawns and manages multiple node sessions with the cluster module.

Getting ready

For this recipe, we will use the sticky session npm module. This can be installed by running `npm install sticky-session`.

How to do it...

To create a Node server using sticky session, follow these steps:

1. Begin by requiring your dependencies. This will include the sticky session module and cluster that is installed along with the node. We will use `cluster` to determine whether our server is the parent or a child process that has been spawned by the parent. Here are the server-side dependencies:

   ```
   var sticky = require('sticky-session'),
       http = require('http'),
       express = require('express'),
       socketIO = require('socket.io'),
       cluster = require('cluster');
   ```

2. Now, call the `sticky()` function and create your app in the function that you pass as your first argument. Anything that is passed to the `sticky()` function will only be executed by children, as shown in the following code:

   ```
   var server = sticky(function() {
     var app = express(), io;

     server = http.Server(app);
     io = socketIO(server);

     // Add your socket.IO connection logic here
     return server;

   });
   ```

3. Now we can start the server that we returned from the `sticky()` function. When we start the server, we should see a master server and multiple child servers logging their greetings to the console, as shown in the following code:

   ```
   server.listen(5000, function() {
     if (cluster.isMaster) {
       console.log('Master server started on port 5000');
     } else {
       console.log('- Child server started on port 5000');
     }
   });
   ```

How it works...

By default, Socket.IO performs multiple requests to create a handshake and a connection to the client. In a distributed environment, each request has the potential to land on a different worker than the previous request. This will break the handshake protocol. As a result, Socket.IO will not work.

The sticky sessions module will be able to get around this issue by always routing the client to the same worker, based on the client's IP address. This guarantees that each new request will land on the same worker. As a result, everything will work as expected.

Using Redis to pass events between nodes

Now that we are able to run multiple nodes simultaneously with Socket.IO and not loose our socket connection between events, we will also need a way to ensure that, when an event is emitted on one node, it is also emitted across all of our other nodes.

For this, Socket.IO uses an interface called an adapter to route messages, and it allows us to use something other than the default memory-based adapter, so we can use our own instead. For a distributed system, we will need to use an adapter that lives outside of our server nodes.

Redis is a perfect solution for this problem. Redis is a key-value store, and cache is stored outside the web servers. This means that we can spin the instances of the server up and down. As a result, the data that is stored in Redis will not be lost. By plugging Redis into our Socket.IO adapter, we can propagate events across our nodes rather painlessly.

Getting ready

First, we will need to have an instance of Redis running. Redis can be downloaded from `http://redis.io`.

There is a very capable `npm` package called `socket.io-redis` that we can use to pass as our adapter. This can be installed from `npm` with the following code:

```
npm install socket.io-redis -save
```

We will also need the Socket.IO emitter to help propagate our events across servers, as shown in the following code:

```
npm install socket.io-emitter --save
```

How to do it...

Follow these steps to pass events between nodes using Redis:

1. First, we will need to include the `socket.io-redis` NPM package on our server and pass our configuration to it with the following code:

```
var redisConfig = {
      host: 'localhost',
      port: 6379
    }, server, io;

var express = require('express'),
    http = require('http'),
    socketIO = require('socket.io'),
    redis = require('socket.io-redis'),
    emitter = require('socket.io-emitter')(redisConfig),
    app = express();
```

2. To test that this works, we should be able to run our server on multiple ports. This allows you to emit and check the message on one port in order to make sure that it has successfully propagated to every other port that is listening for the same event. This can be accomplished with an environmental variable that allows you to dynamically set the port number that we will listen to. The environmental variables in node can be accessed by using the `process.env` object, as shown in the following code:

```
if (!process.env.PORT) {
  throw new Error('Please specify a PORT number, ie:
PORT=5000 node server');
}

app.get('/', function (req, res) {
    res.sendFile(__dirname + '/index.html');
});

server = http.Server(app);
server.listen(process.env.PORT);
```

3. Now, listen for a `message.sent` event from the server and use the `socket.io-emitter` NPM package to emit the event to every socket on any server that we have been listening to for our Redis instance.

```
io = socketIO(server);
io.adapter(redis(redisConfig));
```

```
io.on('connection', function (socket) {
  socket.on('message.sent', function (port) {
    emitter.emit('message.received', port);
  });
});
```

4. Next, we need to add a template on the client side. This template will be responsible for emitting messages to the server with the port number the message originates from. The template will also add an item to the list of messages any time a message comes from the server. We will print the port number in the list to prove that we are affectively communicating with Socket.IO across multiple server instances, as shown in the following code:

```
<div id="messages"></div>

<button id="broadcast">Broadcast</button>

<script src="/socket.io/socket.io.js"></script>
<script>

// The port number needs to be dynamic so we can
// Use this page on any port
var port = window.location.port,
    socket = io.connect('http://localhost:' + port);

// Add new messages to the list
socket.on('message.received', function (port) {
  var message = document.createElement('div');
  message.innerHTML = `Received message from port ${port}`;
  document.getElementById('messages').appendChild(message);
});

// When the "broadcast" button is clicked,
// We will send a message to the server to render the
message
document.getElementById('broadcast').addEventListener('clic
k', function () {
  socket.emit('message.sent', port);
});

</script>
```

5. To test that everything worked as expected, we need to start at least two servers listening on completely separate ports. This can be achieved by passing the environmental variables before the command run Node. In one terminal window, run `PORT=5000 node server`. In a separate terminal window, run `PORT=5001 node server`.
6. Navigate to each of your two servers and click on the **Broadcast** button to send messages. You should see the messages for each port on both servers, even though they are completely separate processes. The output will look something like the following screenshot:

Received message from port 5000
Received message from port 5001
Received message from port 5001
Received message from port 5001
Broadcast

How it works...

In our application, when we receive an event on the server side, we will emit an event to `emitter` instead of `io.sockets`. The emitter is responsible for taking our event and setting it in Redis. The Redis adapter reacts to changes by performing `io.sockets.emit()` on each of our servers behind the scenes.

Redis is essentially its own server, which multiple other servers can access to set and get data from the exposed key-value storage. Typically, Redis is responsible for caching and persisting data that may not need to be in the persistent database. This is often limited to session information, but, in our case, we will use it to set the information that the sockets will emit from the client.

Fortunately, the Redis adapter for Socket.IO already handles all the complicated internals of reacting to newly available data in the Redis data store and propagating it across multiple server instances.

Although there are many ways to use Socket.IO with multiple load-balanced servers, the Redis adapter definitely makes it the easiest approach to handling multiple server instances.

Using Memcached to manage multiple nodes

Memcached is an in-memory key-value store designed to handle small chunks of arbitrary data. Typically, Memcached is used for caching the server and API responses in the memory so that we can render the cached data, instead of hitting the database and waiting for a response if the data has already been persisted in the cache.

Similar to Redis, Memcached is run in a separate server instance out of the web server. This means that we can use it in the same way that we used Redis to propagate events across multiple server nodes.

There are a couple of projects on GitHub with the intention of providing the ability to use Memcached with Socket.IO, but at the time of writing there was none that had been updated after the 1.0 release of Socket.IO. As a result, the implementations all appeared to be either incomplete or buggy. The good news is that the lack of quality Memcached Socket.IO adapters have will provide us with an opportunity to explore how we can use Memcached in our project at a lower level.

Getting ready

For this recipe, we will need to install Memcached on our machine or run it remotely from a service (such as Heroku). The latest version of Memcached can be downloaded from their website at `http://www.memcached.org/downloads`.

We will use the memjs NPM package to access Memcached in Node. This can be installed by running `npm install memjs -save` in your terminal.

How to do it...

To use Memcached to load balance the Socket.IO processes, follow these steps:

1. Create an `adapter.js` file to abstract some of our internal Memcached work. On our server, we will actually require this file instead of Socket.IO itself. Basically, we will overwrite a few Socket.IO methods to get it to send data to Memcached instead of client-side sockets. We will then ping Memcached on specific intervals to check whether or not there is any new data. If there is, call the default `emit()` method on Socket.IO, which we will pass, as shown in the following code:

```
var memjs = require('memjs'),
    socketIO = require('socket.io'),
    _ = require('lodash');
```

```
function Memcached (uri, options) {

    // Create a Memcached connection
    var client = memjs.Client.create(uri, options);

    // This will be the new io method to use instead
    // of the old one
    return function (server) {

        var io = socketIO(server);

        // We will be overriding the emit function, so
we'll make
        // a copy of it for us to use later on
        var _emit = io.emit.bind(io);

        // This value represents the last time that the
Memcached
        // value was emitted. It will be updated each time
there
        // is new data.
        var _lasttime = new Date().getTime();

        function processDataFromCached (err, value, key) {

            // If there is no value, or it can't be parsed
to a
            // string, we need to return it so it doesn't
            // break everything
            if (!value || !value.toString()) {
                return;
            }

            // Parse the data back from a string into JSON
            value = JSON.parse(value && value.toString());

            // If the data has not been emitted on this
server
            if (value.time > _lasttime) {

                // Update the time stamp
                _lasttime = value.time;
```

```
                // Emit the new data using the real
                // socket.io emit function
                _emit(value.topic, value.value);
            }
        }

        function checkDataCache () {

            // Get the socket.io key from Memcached
            client.get('socket.io', processDataFromCached);
        }

        // We will intercept the default behavior of the
emit
        // function. Not to worry, though. We are holding
onto the
        // real socket.io emit function and calling it
_emit. We
        // will call the _emit function when we check the
cache
        // and notice a change
        io.emit = function (topic, value) {
            client.set('socket.io', JSON.stringify({
                topic: topic,
                value: value,

                // We will use the time stamp to compare to
the
                // last time the cache was updated. If it
is newer
                // than the value of _lasttime, we will
emit the
                // new change
                time: new Date().getTime()
            }));
        };

        // Check the cache on an interval to see if there
is a
        // new message
        setInterval(checkDataCache, 500);

        // Return our modified io object
```

```
        return io;
    }

}

module.exports = Memcached;
```

2. The `consumer.js` file will be responsible for consuming the adapter and using it to emit events across multiple servers. We will export the entire consumer as a function so that we can pass a port number to start the server. You can also see that `MEMCACHED_URI`, `MEMCACHED_USERNAME`, and `MEMCACHED_PASSWORD` are being pulled from the environmental variables. Therefore, you will need to create these variables to connect them to the correct instance of Memcached, as follows:

```
module.exports = function (port) {

    var express = require('express'),
        http = require('http'),
        socketIO = require('./adapter')
(process.env.MEMCACHED_URI, {
            username: process.env.MEMCACHED_USERNAME,
            password: process.env.MEMCACHED_PASSWORD
        }),
        app = express();

    console.log('Starting server on port ' + port);

    app.use(express.static(__dirname));

    var server = http.Server(app);
    server.listen(port);

    var io = socketIO(server);

    io.on('connection', function (socket) {
      socket.on('message.sent', function (port) {
        io.emit('message.received', port);
      });
    });

};
```

3. The `server.js` file will be extremely simple. It will just instantiate a couple of the consumers on different ports, as follows:

```
var consumer = require('./consumer');

consumer(5555);
consumer(5556);
```

4. Now, we will create an `index.html` file. This will load a couple of IFrames on the two port numbers that we will run our servers on. This way, we can see both servers interacting in real time. Note that there are various ways to get around cross-domain issues with IFrames these days. Going through WebSockets that communicate through a load-balanced data store is probably not the ideal way to pull it off, but it is an interesting exercise. Use the following code:

```
<!DOCTYPE html>
<html>
  <head>
    <meta charset="utf-8">
    <title>Memcached</title>
    <style media="screen">
        body {
            margin: 0px;
            padding: 0px;
        }
        iframe {
            width: 45%;
            height: 600px;
            border: 0px;
        }
    </style>
  </head>
  <body>
      <iframe src="http://localhost:5555/iframe.html"></iframe>
      <iframe src="http://localhost:5556/iframe.html"></iframe>
  </body>
</html>
```

5. Now, we will need our `index.html` files to render messages that come and broadcast messages. This enables you to prove that you are indeed communicating on multiple Socket.IO instances across multiple servers, as shown in the following code:

```
<!DOCTYPE html>
<html>
```

```
  <head>
    <meta charset="utf-8">
    <title>Memcached</title>
  </head>
  <body>

    <h1>This iframe is on port #<span id="port-
number"></span></h1>

    <div id="messages"></div>

    <hr>

    <button id="broadcast">Broadcast</button>

    <script src="/socket.io/socket.io.js"></script>
    <script>

    // The port number needs to be dynamic so we can
    // Use this page on any port
    var port = window.location.port,
        socket = io.connect('http://localhost:' + port);

    document.getElementById('port-number').innerHTML =
port;

    // Add new messages to the list
    socket.on('message.received', function (port) {
      var message = document.createElement('div');
      message.innerHTML = `Received message from port
${port}`;
      document.getElementById('messages').appendChild(message);
    });

    // When the "broadcast" button is clicked,
    // We will send a message to the server to render the
message
    document.getElementById('broadcast').addEventListener('clic
k', function () {
      socket.emit('message.sent', port);
    });

    </script>
  </body>
</html>
```

6. Now, start your server by running `node server`. You can navigate to the `5555` localhost in your browser and click on the **Broadcast** button in IFrame to broadcast a message in both domains. The result should look similar to the following screenshot:

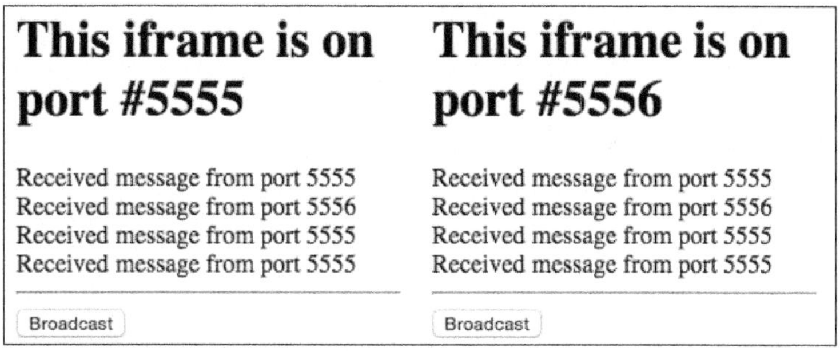

This iframe is on port #5555	This iframe is on port #5556
Received message from port 5555 Received message from port 5556 Received message from port 5555 Received message from port 5555	Received message from port 5555 Received message from port 5556 Received message from port 5555 Received message from port 5555
Broadcast	Broadcast

How it works...

The premise that we will use is actually fairly simple. We will set data on a server instance outside of our web servers so that all of our web servers have access to it. We can then check the data on each of our web servers and determine whether or not anything has updated since the last time we checked the server for the new data. Although we will use Memcached for this, it could really be used for any in-memory data store that doesn't reside on our web server.

Using RabbitMQ to message events across nodes

RabbitMQ is a message-oriented middleware that implements **Advanced Message Queuing Protocol** (**AMQP**) for extremely robust messaging across a distributed system.

In this recipe, we will use RabbitMQ, which allows you to use multiple servers and broadcast messages across them. One big advantage that RabbitMQ holds in comparison to Memcached (for instance) for this sort of task is that it is actually meant to be used to publish or subscribe style events. This means that we won't have to ping a server to determine whether or not there are changes; RabbitMQ will emit changes as they happen, which makes RabbitMQ a perfect solution for the existing style of Socket.IO.

At the time of writing, there were no satisfactory open source RabbitMQ adapters for Socket. IO. This means that we will need to write our own abstraction.

Getting ready

For this recipe, we will need to install RabbitMQ and have it running locally on our machine. It can be installed from `https://www.rabbitmq.com/download.html`.

There are a few officially supported RabbitMQ clients for Java, C#, and Erlang, but for Node, we will have to settle for one that wasn't created by RabbitMQ. One package that works perfectly for this is `amqplib`. It can be installed from NPM by running `npm install amqplib -save`.

How to do it...

In order to use RabbitMQ for message events across nodes, follow these steps:

1. First, we will need to create an `adapter.js` file. This will be an abstraction around Socket.IO. We will override the `emit()` function, but leave the rest of the Socket.IO behavior untouched. When an event is emitted, we will emit it to RabbitMQ instead of sending it directly to the client. We will listen for an event from RabbitMQ so that whenever an event is triggered from any server, every other server will receive the event and will be able to emit the event by using the standard Socket.IO `emit()` method, as shown in the following code:

```
var amqp = require('amqplib'),
    socketIO = require('socket.io'),
    _ = require('lodash');

function RabbitMQ (uri, options) {

    // This will become a reference to the RabbitMQ
connection
    var client;

    // This will be the new io method to use instead of the
    // old one
    return function (server) {

        var io = socketIO(server);

        // We will be overriding the emit function, so
we'll make
        // a copy of it for us to use later on
        var _emit = io.emit.bind(io);
```

```
        function processDataFromCached (message) {

            // If there is no value, or it can't be parsed
to a
            // string, we need to return it so it doesn't
            // break everything
            if (!message || !message.content) {
                return;
            }

            // Parse the data back from a string into
            // a JSON object
            var value =
JSON.parse(message.content.toString());

            // Emit the new data using the real socket.io
            // emit function
            _emit(value.topic, value.value);

            // Ack it back to the RabbitMQ que
            client.ack(message);
        }

        // We will intercept the default behavior of the
emit
        // function. Not to worry, though. We are holding
onto the
        // real socket.io emit function and calling it
_emit. We
        // will call the _emit function when we check the
cache
        // and notice a change
        io.emit = function (topic, value) {

            if (!client) {
                return console.warn('The RabbitMQ channel
is not available...');
            }

            // Loop over the ports to emit to
            _.each(options.sendTo, function (portNumber) {
                client.sendToQueue('socket.io', new
Buffer(JSON.stringify({
                    topic: topic,
```

```
                    value: value
                }))));
            });

        };

        // Create a RabbitMQ connection
        amqp.connect(uri).then(function(connection) {

            // Create a channel from the connection

    connection.createChannel().then(function(channel) {

                // Store a reference to the channel to
                // use on the outside
                client = channel;

                // Listen for events on the que
                client.assertQueue('socket.io', {
                    durable: false
                }).then(function () {

                    // Consume new events
                    client.consume('socket.io',
    processDataFromCached);

                });
            });
        });

        // Return our modified io object
        return io;
    }

}

module.exports = RabbitMQ;
```

2. The `consumer.js` file will give us the ability to start a server with a specified port that we can pass. This way, we can start multiple servers at once from the same process, as follows:

```
module.exports = function (port) {
```

```
    var express = require('express'),
        http = require('http'),
        socketIO = require('./adapter')('amqp://localhost',
{
            sendTo: [5555, 5556]
        }),
        app = express();

    console.log('Starting server on port ' + port);

    app.use(express.static(__dirname));

    var server = http.Server(app);
    server.listen(port);

    var io = socketIO(server);

    io.on('connection', function (socket) {
      socket.on('message.sent', function (port) {
        io.emit('message.received', port);
      });
    });

};
```

3. The `server.js` file will just be responsible for starting some servers by passing the port numbers to the consumer, as shown in the following code:

```
var consumer = require('./consumer');

consumer(5555);
consumer(5556);
```

4. The `index.html` file will be a wrapper to hold some IFrames that will be able to communicate between cross-domain and cross-server, by using RabbitMQ, as shown in the following code:

```
<!DOCTYPE html>
<html>
  <head>
    <meta charset="utf-8">
    <title>Memcached</title>
    <style media="screen">
        body {
            margin: 0px;
```

```
            padding: 0px;
        }
        iframe {
            width: 45%;
            height: 600px;
            border: 0px;
        }
    </style>
  </head>
  <body>
      <iframe
src="http://localhost:5555/iframe.html"></iframe>
      <iframe
src="http://localhost:5556/iframe.html"></iframe>
  </body>
</html>
```

5. Finally, the `iframe.html` file will be in charge of emitting events to the server and displaying messages when events are emitted from the server, as shown in the following code:

```
<!DOCTYPE html>
<html>
  <head>
    <meta charset="utf-8">
    <title>Memcached</title>
  </head>
  <body>

    <h1>This iframe is on port #<span id="port-
number"></span></h1>

    <div id="messages"></div>

    <hr>

    <button id="broadcast">Broadcast</button>

    <script src="/socket.io/socket.io.js"></script>
    <script>

    // The port number needs to be dynamic so we can
    // Use this page on any port
    var port = window.location.port,
        socket = io.connect('http://localhost:' + port);
```

```
    document.getElementById('port-number').innerHTML =
port;

    // Add new messages to the list
    socket.on('message.received', function (port) {
      var message = document.createElement('div');
      message.innerHTML = `Received message from port
${port}`;
      document.getElementById('messages').appendChild(message);
    });

    // When the "broadcast" button is clicked,
    // We will send a message to the server to render the
message
    document.getElementById('broadcast').addEventListener('clic
k', function () {
      socket.emit('message.sent', port);
    });

    </script>
  </body>
</html>
```

6. Now, start your server by running `node server`. You can navigate to the `5555` localhost on your browser and click the **Broadcast** button in the IFrame to broadcast a message in both domains. The result should look similar to the one in the previous recipe.

How it works...

Although RabbitMQ does such a great job of consuming and broadcasting events, this whole process is actually really easy. In our application, Socket.IO will emit a message from the client to the server. Then, the server will take the emitted event and emit it to RabbitMQ. Every server is listening for RabbitMQ to broadcast a Socket.IO message, so, when it does, every server consumes the message and broadcasts it by using the default Socket.IO `emit()` method.

7

Streaming Binary Data

In this chapter, we will cover the following recipes:

- Broadcasting an image to other sockets
- Uploading an image to the filesystem
- Uploading an image to Amazon S3
- Streaming audio
- Streaming live video

Introduction

Socket.IO 1.0 gives us the ability to stream binary data between the server and the client. In this chapter, we will use this ability to transport various forms of binary data, such as images, audio, and video.

Broadcasting an image to other sockets

Typically, the `src` attribute for an HTML image tag will be a link to the location of the image. However, instead of a link to the image, we can actually provide the binary data for the image itself. This ability allows us to store and load actual images and not just the link to the image location.

We can actually use Socket.IO to send images from a browser to a server and then display them in another browser without ever storing them on a server, in a filesystem, or in a database of any kind. In instances where we don't need the data to be stored, this can be really useful.

In this recipe, we will demonstrate how we can pipe an image from our filesystem to the browser over WebSockets.

Getting ready...

In this recipe, I will use a static image called `woodchuck.jpg` to pipe into the browser. It is located at the root of the app along with the `server.js` and `index.html` files. You should be able to put any image that you want to use in that location as long as you reference the correct image in your server code. As new chunks of the image are read, they will be emitted to the browser using the `image-chunk` event.

How to do it...

To broadcast images over Socket.IO, follow these steps:

1. First, we will create our `server.js` file. This file will wait for the socket connection event and immediately begin to read the image by creating a read stream using the built-in `fs` module that comes with Node:

```
var express = require('express'),
app = express(),
http = require('http'),
socketIO = require('socket.io'),
fs = require('fs'),
path = require('path'),
server, io;

app.get('/', function (req, res) {
res.sendFile(__dirname + '/index.html');
});

server = http.Server(app);
server.listen(5000);

io = socketIO(server);

io.on('connection', function (socket) {
varreadStream = fs.createReadStream(path.resolve(__dirname, './
woodchuck.jpg'), {
encoding: 'binary'
    }), chunks = [];
```

```
readStream.on('readable', function () {
console.log('Image loading');
    });

readStream.on('data', function (chunk) {
chunks.push(chunk);
socket.emit('img-chunk', chunk);
    });

readStream.on('end', function () {
console.log('Image loaded');
    });
});
```

2. Now, we need to create an `index.html` page to render the image in pieces as data is chunked in:

```
<!DOCTYPE html>
<html>
<head>
<meta charset="utf-8">
<title></title>
</head>
<body>
<img id="img-stream2" src="" />
<scriptsrc="/socket.io/socket.io.js"></script>
<script type="text/javascript">
var socket = io.connect('http://localhost:5000');

varimgChunks = [];

socket.on('img-chunk', function (chunk) {
var img = document.getElementById('img-stream2');
imgChunks.push(chunk);
img.setAttribute('src', 'data:image/jpeg;base64,' + window.
btoa(imgChunks));
        });
</script>
</body>
</html>
```

3. Start your server and go to `localhost:5000`. The image will be rendered. If you view the element in your developer console, you should see that it is prefixed with **data:image/jpeg;base64**, followed by a base64-encoded string:

How it works...

When a user connects to our server, we immediately begin to read the contents of the image file using a read stream. This allows us to emit parts of the image as they are read instead of emitting it all at once. This means the image will load progressively as the data is chunked.

There's more...

If you are on a fast connection, you may not notice that the image is loading in pieces. The best way to demonstrate that it is loading progressively is to set a timeout to delay the loading of each part of the image for a set amount of time, as shown here:

```
var delay = 0;
readStream.on('data', function (chunk) {
chunks.push(chunk);
delay = delay + 5000;
setTimeout(function () {
socket.emit('img-chunk', chunk);
    }, delay);
});
```

Uploading an image to the filesystem

With Socket.IO, we can send files to our server over WebSockets instead of using an `http POST` request. Socket.IO allows us to upload files in real time and display the uploaded images as needed.

In this recipe, we will use Socket.IO to upload a file to our local filesystem and then send a message to the client to display the image when it is done uploading.

Getting ready...

For this recipe, we will use the built-in Node `fs` module to upload our images.

We will upload files to our filesystem, so make sure that you create a folder called `tmp` in the root of your project.

How to do it...

To upload an image to the filesystem with Socket.IO, follow these steps:

1. First, we will need to create our `server.js` file. This file will be responsible for listening for new `upload-image` messages and uploading the file that is passed with the arguments:

```
var express = require('express'),
app = express(),
http = require('http'),
socketIO = require('socket.io'),
fs = require('fs'),
path = require('path'),
server, io;

app.use(express.static(__dirname));

server = http.Server(app);
server.listen(5000);

console.log('Listening on port 5000');

io = socketIO(server);

io.on('connection', function (socket) {
socket.on('upload-image', function (message) {
```

```
var writer = fs.createWriteStream(path.resolve(__dirname, './tmp/'
+ message.name), {
encoding: 'base64'
        });


writer.write(message.data);
writer.end();

writer.on('finish', function () {

socket.emit('image-uploaded', {
name: '/tmp/' + message.name
            });

        });

    });
});
```

2. Finally, we need to create an `index.html` template for our client side. We will add a `change` event to listen for an item being selected in the input field and read the file and emit it when the event is triggered:

```
<!DOCTYPE html>
<html>
<head>
<meta charset="utf-8">
<title></title>
</head>
<body>

<hr />
<input type="file" id="my-file" />
<hr />

<scriptsrc="/socket.io/socket.io.js"></script>
<script type="text/javascript">
var socket = io.connect('http://localhost:5000');

var file = document.getElementById('my-file');
```

```
file.addEventListener('change', function () {
if (!file.files.length) {
return;
            }

varfirstFile = file.files[0],
reader = new FileReader();

reader.onloadend = function () {
socket.emit('upload-image', {
name: firstFile.name,
data: reader.result
                });
            };

reader.readAsArrayBuffer(firstFile);
        });

socket.on('image-uploaded', function (message) {
varimg = document.createElement('img');
img.setAttribute('src', message.name);
img.setAttribute('height', '100px');
document.body.appendChild(img);
        });
</script>
</body>
</html>
```

3. Now, if you start your server and go to `localhost:5000/index.html`, you should see an input field for uploading a file to the server. Just choose a file and it will upload to your `/tmp` directory and display the following file input:

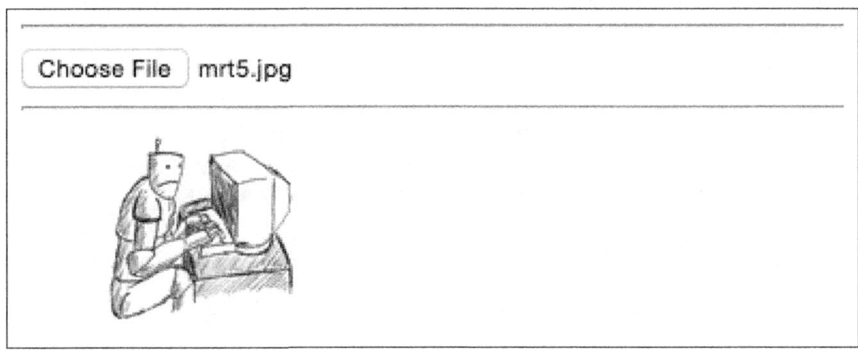

How it works...

Socket.IO can pass any kind of data, including binary file data. Our client-side JavaScript allows us to access the file using the `FileReader()` API. We can pass the data we extract from the FileReader to the server and let the server write the file. When the file is added to the filesystem, the server emits a message to let us know that the upload is complete. At that point, we can display the newly-uploaded file on the client.

Uploading an image to Amazon S3

Uploading images to your server-side filesystem is actually not a great idea. If you are deploying from your repo, you don't want to mix in user-generated media with your code. A much better and more scalable approach is to put your photos and other media in a completely separate static location, such as Amazon S3, where you can access them without letting them interfere with your core application.

In this recipe, we will upload images to Amazon S3 and display them after they are uploaded.

Getting ready...

For this recipe, we will use the Amazon SDK for Node. It can be installed by running `npm install aws-sdk -save` in your terminal. We will also use lodash (`npm install lodash --save`) and the `q` promise library (`npm install q --save`).

How to do it...

To upload an image to Amazon S3, follow these steps:

1. First, we will create an `aws.service.js` file. This file will be responsible for interfacing with the Amazon AWS SDK and writing and reading binary data from Amazon. We will use some environmental variables that we will need to set by exporting them in our terminal; for example, `export AWS_ACCESS_KEY_ID="AKGAJ2PTGPBP3GAIPZ7G`. The required environmental variables are `AWS_ACCESS_KEY_ID`, which is the key to your Amazon account; `AWS_SECRET_ACCESS_KEY`, which is the secret key for your Amazon account; `AWS_BUCKET_NAME`, which is the name of the bucket you have set up on Amazon that you want to write to; and `AWS_BUCKET_PATH`, which is the path that you want your files to be written to:

```
var AWS = require('aws-sdk'),
    _ = require('lodash'),
q = require('q');

var service = {}, s3;
```

```
var AWS_ACCESS_KEY_ID = process.env.AWS_ACCESS_KEY_ID,
    AWS_SECRET_ACCESS_KEY = process.env.AWS_SECRET_ACCESS_KEY,
    AWS_BUCKET_NAME = process.env.AWS_BUCKET_NAME,
    AWS_BUCKET_PATH = process.env.AWS_BUCKET_PATH;

AWS.config.update({
accessKeyId: AWS_ACCESS_KEY_ID,
secretAccessKey: AWS_SECRET_ACCESS_KEY
});

s3 = new AWS.S3();

function write (path, file) {
vardeffered = q.defer();

s3.putObject({
        Bucket: AWS_BUCKET_NAME,
        Key: AWS_BUCKET_PATH + '/' + path,
        Body: file
    }, function (err, data) {
deffered.resolve(data || err);
    });

returndeffered.promise;
}

functionreadFile (path) {
vardeffered = q.defer();

path = path.replace(AWS_BUCKET_PATH + '/', '');

s3.getObject({
        Bucket: AWS_BUCKET_NAME,
        Key: AWS_BUCKET_PATH + '/' + path
    }, function (err, data) {
if (!data) {
deffered.resolve(err);
        } else {
deffered.resolve(_.extend(data, {
path: path
            }));
        }
    });
```

```
returndeffered.promise;
}

function read (path) {
vardeffered = q.defer();

readFile(path).then(function (data) {
if (data.Body) {
varbuf = new Buffer(data.Body);
deffered.resolve(buf.toString());
        } else {
deffered.resolve(null);
        }
    });

returndeffered.promise;
}

module.exports = {
write: write,
read: read,
readFile: readFile
};
```

2. The `server.js` file will be responsible for listening for Socket.IO events and uploading the images as they come in via the AWS service that we created. After each file is uploaded, we will read it as a base64-encoded string and emit the result back to the client so that the client can display the image:

```
var express = require('express'),
app = express(),
http = require('http'),
socketIO = require('socket.io'),
fs = require('fs'),
path = require('path'),
aws = require('./aws.service'),
server, io;

app.use(express.static(__dirname));

app.get('/', function (req, res) {
res.sendFile(__dirname + '/index.html');
});

server = http.Server(app);
```

```
server.listen(5000);

console.log('Listening on port 5000');

io = socketIO(server);

io.on('connection', function (socket) {
socket.on('upload-image', function (message) {
var path = 'socketio/' + message.name;

aws.write(path, message.data).then(function (response) {
returnaws.readFile(path);
        }).then(function (response) {

var base64 = response.Body.toString('base64');

socket.emit('image-uploaded', {
name: 'data:image/jpeg;base64,' +  base64
            });

        });

    });
});
```

3. Now, we need to add the client-side `index.html` file. This file will be responsible for reading files with the `FileReader()` method and sending the file data to the server with Socket.IO:

```
<!DOCTYPE html>
<html>
<head>
<meta charset="utf-8">
<title></title>
</head>
<body>

<hr />
<input type="file" id="my-file" />
<hr />

<scriptsrc="/socket.io/socket.io.js"></script>
<script type="text/javascript">
var socket = io.connect('http://localhost:5000');
```

```
var file = document.getElementById('my-file');

file.addEventListener('change', function () {
if (!file.files.length) {
return;
            }

varfirstFile = file.files[0],
reader = new FileReader();

reader.onloadend = function () {
socket.emit('upload-image', {
name: firstFile.name,
data: reader.result
                });
            };

reader.readAsArrayBuffer(firstFile);
        });

socket.on('image-uploaded', function (message) {
varimg = document.createElement('img');
img.setAttribute('src', message.name);
img.setAttribute('height', '100px');
document.body.appendChild(img);
        });
</script>
</body>
</html>
```

4. Now, start your server and go to `localhost:5000/index.html`. You should be able to upload a file to AWS and see the results render below the upload input.

How it works...

When we upload binary image data to the server with Socket.IO, we call the `aws.write()` function to save data to AWS. The service hides most of the business logic involved in writing files to Amazon so that the Socket.IO requests and responses are able to stay slim. This service also makes the AWS reading and writing functions reusable for other endpoints to call.

The AWS SDK provides methods to read, write, listen to, and delete files, so we are able to use these methods in our service to pass files to Amazon. As long as our environmental variables are set correctly and we are sending files to Amazon S3, everything should work.

Streaming audio

Streaming images with Socket.IO is great. However, we can use WebSockets in combination with WebRTC to stream audio from one user's microphone to another.

WebRTC (**Web Real-Time Communication**) is an API that supports browser-to-browser real-time media sharing for applications such as voice calling, video chat, and peer-to-peer file sharing. WebRTC is still a relatively new technology. While WebRTC has support in most browsers, at the time of writing this book, Internet Explorer and Safari do not yet support it.

For two browsers to directly communicate over WebRTC, there is a handshake process that needs to take place. This means that one client makes an offer containing a description of the offer. The second client must then accept the offer and pass a reciprocal description. When the first client receives the answer to their offer, it must set the remote description that is contained in the offer answer. At that point, both clients have agreed to create a WebRTC connection, and they are free to openly communicate.

Socket.IO is an ideal candidate for sending offers and answers to the offers before the connection is securely established.

In this recipe, we will use Socket.IO to help establish a WebRTC connection so that we can transmit live audio from one browser to another.

How to do it...

To stream audio with WebRTC and Socket.IO, follow these steps:

1. First, we will create our `server.js` file. This file will be responsible for facilitating the connection of two clients such that they can communicate with WebRTC:

```
var express = require('express'),
app = express(),
http = require('http'),
socketIO = require('socket.io'),
server, io;

app.use(express.static(__dirname));

server = http.Server(app);
server.listen(5000);

console.log('Listening on port 5000');

io = socketIO(server);
```

```
io.on('connection', function (socket) {

socket.on('make-offer', function (data) {
socket.broadcast.emit('offer-made', {
offer: data.offer,
socket: socket.id
        });
    });

socket.on('make-answer', function (data) {
socket.to(data.to).emit('answer-made', {
socket: socket.id,
answer: data.answer
        });
    });

});
```

2. Now, we will create our `sender.html` file. This file will simply display a button to broadcast our audio to the other client:

```
<!DOCTYPE html>
<html>
<head>
<meta charset="utf-8">
<title></title>
<linkrel="stylesheet" href="/style.css" media="screen"
charset="utf-8" />
</head>
<body>
<button id="broadcast" class="play">Broadcast</button>

<scriptsrc="/socket.io/socket.io.js"></script>
<script type="text/javascript" src="/shared.js"></script>
<script type="text/javascript" src="/sender.js"></script>
</body>
</html>
```

3. Since we will create two separate pages, we will use a `shared.js` file to include common variables and functions that both pages can use. This file will mostly allow the WebRTC variables to fall back on browser vendor prefixes, since support for the unprefixed namespaces is still spotty. We will also create our own peer connection to transmit data:

```
varpeerConnection = window.RTCPeerConnection ||
window.mozRTCPeerConnection ||
```

```
window.webkitRTCPeerConnection ||
window.msRTCPeerConnection;

varsessionDescription = window.RTCSessionDescription ||
window.mozRTCSessionDescription ||
window.webkitRTCSessionDescription ||
window.msRTCSessionDescription;

navigator.getUserMedia  = navigator.getUserMedia ||
navigator.webkitGetUserMedia ||
navigator.mozGetUserMedia ||
navigator.msGetUserMedia;

var socket = io.connect('http://localhost:5000');

var pc = new peerConnection({ iceServers: [{ url: 'stun:stun.
services.mozilla.com',
username: 'myuser',
credential: 'mycreds'
 }]
});

function error (err) {
console.warn(err);
}
```

4. Now, we will need a `sender.js` file to pair with our `sender.html` template. This file will allow the user to click on the **Broadcast** button to establish a peer-to-peer connection with other clients and stream data once the connection is created:

```
varanswersFrom = {};

navigator.getUserMedia({ audio: true }, function (stream) {
pc.addStream(stream);
}, error);

functioncreateOffer () {
pc.createOffer(function(offer) {
pc.setLocalDescription(new sessionDescription(offer), function ()
{
socket.emit('make-offer', {
offer: offer
            });
        }, error);
    }, error);
```

```
}

socket.on('answer-made', function (data) {
pc.setRemoteDescription(new sessionDescription(data.answer),
function () {
if (!answersFrom[data.socket]) {
createOffer(data.socket);
answersFrom[data.socket] = true;
        }
    }, error);
});

varbtn = document.getElementById('broadcast');
btn.addEventListener('click', function () {
if (btn.getAttribute('class') === 'stop') {
btn.setAttribute('class', 'play');
btn.innerHTML = 'Broadcast';
    } else {
btn.setAttribute('class', 'stop');
btn.innerHTML = 'Broadcasting...';
createOffer();
    }
});
```

5. Now, we will create a `receiver.html` file. Users can go to this file to listen to the stream that will be created in our sender page. The receiver will wait for a connection to be requested by the sender. Then, the user can click on the single button to allow the connection to be created:

```
<!DOCTYPE html>
<html>
<head>
<meta charset="utf-8">
<title></title>
<linkrel="stylesheet" href="/style.css" media="screen"
charset="utf-8" />
</head>
<body>
<button id="btn" class="muted">No Station...</button>

<scriptsrc="/socket.io/socket.io.js"></script>
<script type="text/javascript" src="/shared.js"></script>
<script type="text/javascript" src="/reciever.js"></script>
</body>
</html>
```

6. The `receiver.js` file will handle listening for offers being created in Socket.IO and allow the user to accept the offer and begin streaming the audio feed from the sender:

```
varofferData,
player = new Audio(),
btn = document.getElementById('btn');

btn.addEventListener('click', function () {
if (btn.getAttribute('class') === 'play') {
listen();
player.play();
    } else if (btn.getAttribute('class') === 'stop') {
player.pause();
btn.setAttribute('class', 'muted');
btn.innerHTML = 'No Station...';
    }
});

function listen () {
btn.setAttribute('class', 'stop');
btn.innerHTML = 'Listening';

pc.setRemoteDescription(new sessionDescription(offerData.offer),
function () {
pc.createAnswer(function (answer) {
pc.setLocalDescription(new sessionDescription(answer), function ()
{
socket.emit('make-answer', {
answer: answer,
to: offerData.socket
                });
            }, error);
          }, error);
    }, error);
}

pc.onaddstream = function (obj) {
console.log('addStream');
player.src = window.URL.createObjectURL(obj.stream);
};

socket.on('offer-made', function (data) {
btn.setAttribute('class', 'play');
btn.innerHTML = 'Listen';
offerData = data;
});
```

7. Finally, we'll add some CSS in a `style.css` file to change the color of our button as needed:

```
button {
font-size: 2em;
border: 0px;
color: #FFF;
}

button.play {
background: green;
}

button.stop {
background: red;
}

button.muted {
background: #CCC;
}
```

8. Now, we can start our server and go to `localhost:5000/sender.html` in one browser and `localhost:5000/receiver.html` in a different browser. When you navigate to the `sender.html` page, it will prompt you to allow the browser to use your microphone. When you enable the microphone and click on the green button, it will make an offer to establish a WebRTC connection with the other browser:

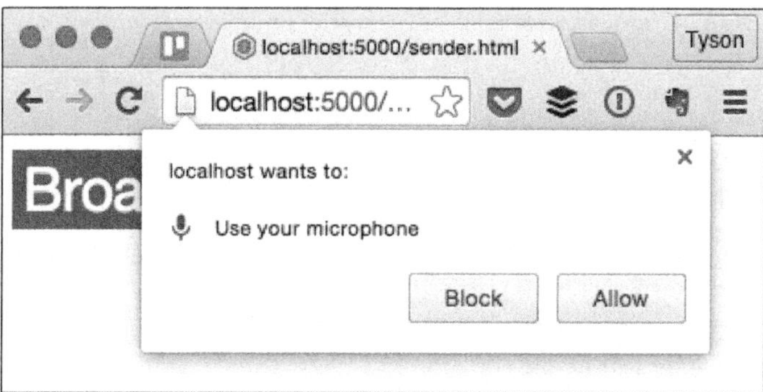

9. At first, `receiver.html` will say that no station is available:

10. However, once the sender initializes the connection, the button will change to read **Listen**:

11. Once the user clicks on the **Listen** button, the connection will be fully established, and they will begin to hear the audio streaming from the sender. Make sure that you wear headphones if your sender and receiver are both being opened on the same computer, or you will get some nasty feedback.

How it works...

WebRTC and WebSockets work together really nicely to create a real-time streaming experience. In our example, we used Socket.IO to facilitate the creation of the connection between our clients, and then we let WebRTC take it from there.

The WebRTC API allowed us to generate session descriptions, which we emitted over Socket.IO to authenticate the two browsers with each other. The descriptions are just basic JavaScript objects with some metadata describing the type of connection we are trying to create, so they are easily transported over WebSockets.

Streaming live video

While streaming audio is great, live video is even more gratifying. Using the WebRTC protocol, we can stream video in addition to audio and simply pipe it into an HTML video element instead of an audio element.

In this recipe, we will create a peer-to-peer connection where we can allow two users to chat using live video.

How to do it...

To stream live video with Socket.IO, follow these steps:

1. First, we need to create a `server.js` file. This file will be responsible for managing sockets as they join or leave. It will also be responsible for allowing the sockets to connect to one another to initiate a WebRTC session:

```
var express = require('express'),
app = express(),
```

```
http = require('http'),
socketIO = require('socket.io'),
fs = require('fs'),
path = require('path'),
server, io, sockets = [];

app.use(express.static(__dirname));

app.get('/', function (req, res) {
res.sendFile(__dirname + '/index.html');
});

server = http.Server(app);
server.listen(5000);

console.log('Listening on port 5000');

io = socketIO(server);

io.on('connection', function (socket) {

socket.emit('add-users', {
users: sockets
    });

socket.broadcast.emit('add-users', {
users: [socket.id]
    });

socket.on('make-offer', function (data) {
socket.to(data.to).emit('offer-made', {
offer: data.offer,
socket: socket.id
        });
    });

socket.on('make-answer', function (data) {
socket.to(data.to).emit('answer-made', {
socket: socket.id,
answer: data.answer
        });
    });
```

```
socket.on('disconnect', function () {
sockets.splice(sockets.indexOf(socket.id), 1);
io.emit('remove-user', socket.id);
    });

sockets.push(socket.id);

});
```

2. Now, we will create the `index.html` template to display our client-side code:

```
<!DOCTYPE html>
<html>
<head>
<meta charset="utf-8">
<title></title>
<linkrel="stylesheet" href="/style.css" media="screen"
charset="utf-8" />
</head>
<body>
<div class="container">
<video class="video-large" autoplay></video>
<div class="users-container" id="users-container">
<h4>Users</h4>
<div id="users"></div>
</div>
<div>

<scriptsrc="/socket.io/socket.io.js"></script>
<script type="text/javascript" src="/index.js"></script>
</body>
</html>
```

3. Next, we will create our `index.js` file, which will include our client-side JavaScript. This file will be responsible for creating new WebRTC connections and responding to WebRTC connection requests from other users:

```
var socket = io.connect('http://localhost:5000');

varanswersFrom = {}, offer;

varpeerConnection = window.RTCPeerConnection ||
window.mozRTCPeerConnection ||
window.webkitRTCPeerConnection ||
window.msRTCPeerConnection;
```

```
varsessionDescription = window.RTCSessionDescription ||
window.mozRTCSessionDescription ||
window.webkitRTCSessionDescription ||
window.msRTCSessionDescription;

navigator.getUserMedia  = navigator.getUserMedia ||
navigator.webkitGetUserMedia ||
navigator.mozGetUserMedia ||
navigator.msGetUserMedia;

var pc = new peerConnection({ iceServers: [{ url: "stun:stun.
services.mozilla.com",
username: "somename",
credential: "somecredentials" }]
});

pc.onaddstream = function (obj) {
var vid = document.createElement('video');
vid.setAttribute('class', 'video-small');
vid.setAttribute('autoplay', 'autoplay');
vid.setAttribute('id', 'video-small');
document.getElementById('users-container').appendChild(vid);
vid.src = window.URL.createObjectURL(obj.stream);
}

navigator.getUserMedia({video: true}, function (stream) {
var video = document.querySelector('video');
video.src = window.URL.createObjectURL(stream);
pc.addStream(stream);
}, error);

function error (err) {
console.warn('Error', err);
}

functioncreateOffer (id) {
pc.createOffer(function(offer) {
pc.setLocalDescription(new sessionDescription(offer), function ()
{
socket.emit('make-offer', {
offer: offer,
to: id
```

```
                });
            }, error);
        }, error);
    }

    socket.on('answer-made', function (data) {
    pc.setRemoteDescription(new sessionDescription(data.answer),
    function () {
    document.getElementById(data.socket).setAttribute('class',
    'active');
    if (!answersFrom[data.socket]) {
    createOffer(data.socket);
    answersFrom[data.socket] = true;
            }
        }, error);
    });

    socket.on('offer-made', function (data) {
    offer = data.offer;

    pc.setRemoteDescription(new sessionDescription(data.offer),
    function () {
    pc.createAnswer(function (answer) {
    pc.setLocalDescription(new sessionDescription(answer), function ()
    {
    socket.emit('make-answer', {
    answer: answer,
    to: data.socket
                });
            }, error);
        }, error);
    }, error);
    });

    socket.on('add-users', function (data) {
    for (vari = 0; i<data.users.length; i++) {
    var el = document.createElement('div'),
    id = data.users[i];

    el.setAttribute('id', id);
    el.innerHTML = id;
    el.addEventListener('click', function () {
    createOffer(id);
```

```
        });
document.getElementById('users').appendChild(el);
    }
});

socket.on('remove-user', function (id) {
var div = document.getElementById(id);
document.getElementById('users').removeChild(div);
});
```

4. Finally, we need to add some CSS in `style.css` to make our page look nice:

```
html, body {
padding: 0px;
margin: 0px;
}

video {
background: #CCC;
}

.container {
width: 100%;
}

.video-large {
width: 75%;
float: left;
}

.users-container {
width: 21%;
float: left;
padding: 2%;
position: relative;
}

.video-small {
margin-top: 20px;
width: 100%;
}
```

```
#users div {
color: red;
text-decoration: underline;
cursor: pointer;
}

#users .active {
color: #000;
cursor: default;
}
```

5. Now, we can navigate to `localhost:5000` in two browsers and click on the user that shows up in the pane on the right-hand side. This will kick off the process of creating a WebRTC video connection using Socket.IO to message the connection description:

How it works...

Most of the magic here is happening through WebRTC. Socket.IO simply handles the handshake process to authenticate the handshake on both ends.

Once the connection is established, we are piping data over the WebRTC connection with the `addStream()` method on the peer connection. We can create a data URL to pass as the `src` of our video element by calling `window.URL.createObjectURL()`. If the WebRTC session is successfully authenticated, the video will stream as expected.

8

Integrating with Mobile Applications

In this chapter, we will cover the following recipes:

- Throwing an alert when the socket connects
- Pushing up data from the server
- Responding to tap events from the device
- Doing server-side pagination
- Triggering hot deploys

Introduction

Socket.IO not only works on websites, but also in native Cordova and Phonegap applications. In this chapter, we will get Socket.IO working in a Cordova application.

Throwing an alert when the socket connects

Apache Cordova is a platform for building native mobile applications using HTML, CSS, and JavaScript. It basically wraps your entire application in a web view and exposes certain native events to the application through JavaScript.

In this recipe, we will emit a message from the server using Socket.IO when the application first opens.

Getting ready

For this recipe, you will need to use a Mac. The reason for this is that Cordova will create an app that runs using XCode, which is only available for the Macintosh operating system.

How to do it...

To throw an alert in a Cordova app when the socket connects, follow these steps:

1. First, we need to install Cordova. There is a command-line interface that can be installed by running `npm install cordova -g` in your terminal.
2. Next, we need to create a new application using the Cordova command-line interface that we just installed. Cordova can be run with `cordova create app com.throw.alertThrowAlert`. The first argument, `app`, will be the folder into which the project gets built into. The second argument, `com.throw.alert`, is the reverse domain-style identifier. The third argument, `ThrowAlert`, is the application title.
3. Now, we will add a platform to our app. Cordova is not limited to running iOS emulations, but it is a good starting point. We can run `cordova platform add ios` to add the iOS platform as a target for our project.
4. Now that we have an iOS target, we can build to it by running `cordova build ios`.
5. What we really want is to be able to emulate an iOS device, and for this we need an iOS simulator. We can install the simulator by running `brew install ios-sim`.
6. Now that we've got Cordova ready to go, we'll need a server to use Socket.IO with. We can create a `server.js` file, as follows, and start it for access in the app:

   ```
   var server = require('http').createServer();
   vario = require('socket.io')(server);

   io.sockets.on('connection', function (socket) {

   console.log('App socket connected');

   socket.emit('alert', 'This app is connected to
   Socket.IO!');
   });

   server.listen(5000);
   ```

7. Now, in the Cordova application that you generated, there will be an `index.html` file located in the `/www` directory. This will be the file that Cordova uses when you navigate to your app on a device. We can add the following lines of code to the index file to start using Socket.IO in our app:

```
<script type="text/javascript" src="cordova.js"></script>
<script type="text/javascript" src=" js/socket.io/socket.io.js"></
script>
<script type="text/javascript" src="js/index.js"></script>
<script type="text/javascript">
app.initialize();

var socket = io('http://localhost:5000');

document.addEventListener('deviceready', function() {

socket.on('connect', function () {
socket.on('alert', function (message) {
alert(message);
            });
        });
    });
</script>
```

8. Now run `cordova emulate ios`. After the app starts, you should see something like this:

How it works...

Unlike standard web pages, applications wrapped in Cordova are not restricted by a cross-domain origin policy. This means that we are able to load Socket.IO from any domain, and it will just work. In our example, we are starting a server on port `5000`, so we simply have to load the script from the same location and call the `io()` function with our first argument pointing to the server and the port we have spun up.

Pushing up data from the server

Using Socket.IO in a Cordova app is exactly the same as using it on a website. We emit events and listen for events. In the mobile device context, one interesting application is using Socket.IO as an interface over a third-party API. When the mobile device uses Socket.IO to kick off requests to the API, it doesn't have to wait for the request to complete. It will simply get a message when this occurs.

In this recipe, we will use Socket.IO as an interface to make a request to the `openweathermap.org` API.

Getting ready

To make request to a third-party API, we will use the request library. It can be installed by running `npm install request` in your command line.

How to do it...

To create a weather app that interfaces with a third-party API, follow these steps:

1. First, we need to create a new Cordova application. This can be done by running `cordova create app com.push.dataPushData` in your command line.
2. Next, add the iOS platform by running `cordova platform add ios`, and build it by running `cordova build ios`.
3. Now, let's create our `server.js` file. This file will just need to listen for requests to get the weather and then respond by hitting the API and emitting an event with the freshly fetched weather data:

```
var server = require('http').createServer(),
io = require('socket.io')(server),
request = require('request');

io.sockets.on('connection', function (socket) {
```

```
// The location will only work in Android if we are using
the location plugin
socket.on('set-location', function (location) {
request('http://api.openweathermap.org/data/2.5/weather?q='
+ location, function (error, response, body) {
if (!error &&response.statusCode == 200) {
socket.emit('weather-change', JSON.parse(body));
            }
        });
    });

});

server.listen(5000);
```

4. Now let's write our app. The `index.html` file will be fairly simple. We just have a form to request the weather for any location and then a section underneath where the response will be rendered. Here is the client side template:

```
<!DOCTYPE html>
<html>
<head>
<meta name="viewport" content="user-scalable=no, initial-
scale=1, maximum-scale=1, minimum-scale=1, width=device-
width">
<linkrel="stylesheet"
href="http://bootswatch.com/superhero/bootstrap.min.css">
<title>Weather</title>
</head>
<body>
<div class="container">
<h1>Weather</h1>
<form id="submit-weather">
<div class="row">
<div class="col-md-12">
<label for="location">Location:</label>
</div>
<div class="col-md-12">
<input id="location" type="text" name="location"
class="form-control" />
</div>
<div class="col-md-12">
<br />
<button type="submit" name="button" class="btnbtn-primary
btn-lgbtn-block">Go</button>
```

```
</div>
</div>
</form>

<h1 id="location-name"></h1>
<h2 id="weather-main"></h2>
<p id="weather-description"></p>
</div>
<script type="text/javascript" src="cordova.js"></script>
<script type="text/javascript"
src="http://localhost:5000/socket.io/socket.io.js"></script
>
<script type="text/javascript" src="js/index.js"></script>
</body>
</html>
```

5. Finally, our client-side `index.js` file will be responsible for submitting the form value to the server over Socket.IO and for listening for an event to render the weather:

```
var socket = io('http://localhost:5000');

document.getElementById('submit-
weather').addEventListener('submit', function (e) {
var location = document.getElementById('location').value;
e.preventDefault();
document.getElementById('location-name').innerHTML =
'Loading...';
socket.emit('set-location', location);
});

socket.on('weather-change', function (data) {
document.getElementById('location-name').innerHTML =
data.name + ' ' +
        ' <imgsrc="http://openweathermap.org/img/w/' +
data.weather[0].icon + '.png">';
document.getElementById('weather-main').innerHTML =
data.weather[0].main;
document.getElementById('weather-description').innerHTML =
data.weather[0].description;
});
```

6. Now, we can run `cordova emulate ios` to see the application in action. It will present us with a form to request the weather for a location and then render the data as it comes back from the weather API:

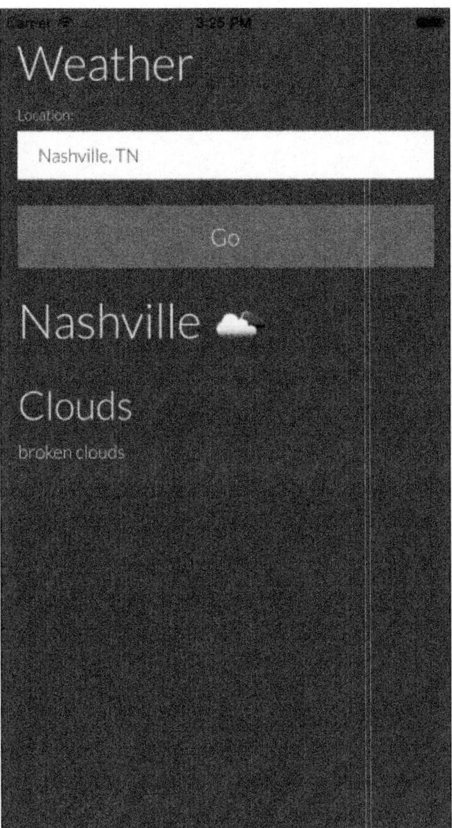

How it works...

We are basically using Socket.IO to create a proxy to interface with an API. We can emit a message to the server to start a request to some other server that we are proxying. At that point, the client side only needs to listen for new data and doesn't have to concern itself with the implementation details of how the data is retrieved. The server finishes grabbing the data from the API and responds, and the client (or multiple clients, if you'd prefer) is able to render the new data.

Responding to tap events from the device

One cool thing about having a central server-side location to emit events from using Socket.IO is that you can use it as an API for multiple applications.

In this recipe, we will emit events to the server every time a user taps on a button on our app. The server will then emit the tap data to the client side, where it will be displayed on an analytics page.

This technique can be useful for gathering analytics data in real time, and watching the results of A/B testing as they happen.

How to do it...

To respond to tap events from the device by updating the counts on our analytics page, follow these steps:

1. First, we will create our new Cordova app by running `cordova create app com.client.tapsclientTaps`.
2. Next, we will add the iOS platform by running `cordova platform add ios`, and build it by running `cordova build ios`.
3. Now, we can create our server. This server will go in `server.js`, and it is only responsible for listening for tap events and emitting the events to any clients that might be listening:

```
var server = require('http').createServer(),
io = require('socket.io')(server);

io.sockets.on('connection', function (socket) {
socket.on('button-tap', function (btn) {
io.sockets.emit('button-tapped', btn);
    });
});

server.listen(5000);
```

4. Now, we will need to create a `dashboard.html` file. This file will go outside our app project because we will just be looking at it in our browser. It will listen for the button-tapped event and update the UI when it is received:

```
<!DOCTYPE html>
<html>
<head>
<linkrel="stylesheet"
href="http://bootswatch.com/paper/bootstrap.min.css">
```

```
<title>Analytics Dashboard</title>
</head>
<body>
<div class="container">
<h1>Analytics Dashboard</h1>
<div class="row">
<div class="col-md-4">
<h2 class="text-primary">Button 1</h2>
<p><span id="btn-1-clicks">0</span> clicks</p>
</div>
<div class="col-md-4">
<h2 class="text-success">Button 2</h2>
<p><span id="btn-2-clicks">0</span> clicks</p>
</div>
<div class="col-md-4">
<h2 class="text-danger">Button 3</h2>
<p><span id="btn-3-clicks">0</span> clicks</p>
</div>
</div>
</div>
<script type="text/javascript"
src="http://localhost:5000/socket.io/socket.io.js"></script
<script type="text/javascript">
var socket = io('http://localhost:5000');

socket.on('button-tapped', function (i) {
var el = document.getElementById(`btn-${i}-clicks`);
el.innerHTML = parseInt(el.innerHTML) + 1;
            });
</script>
</body>
</html>
```

The output will look like the following screenshot:

Analytics Dashboard

Button 1 — 0 clicks

Button 2 — 0 clicks

Button 3 — 0 clicks

5. Now, our `index.html` file inside our Cordova app will just be a list of buttons that can be tapped. When any one of the buttons is tapped, the background color of the app will be changed, and we will send the index of the tapped button to the server. The server will emit it and make it visible to our analytics UI:

```
<!DOCTYPE html>
<html>
<head>
<linkrel="stylesheet" href="http://bootswatch.com/paper/bootstrap.
min.css">
<title>Taps</title>
</head>
<body>
<div class="container">
<h1>What is your favorite color?</h1>
<p>
<button data-id="1" class="btnbtn-primary btn-lgbtn-
block">Blue</button>
</p>
<p>
<button data-id="2" class="btnbtn-success btn-lgbtn-
block">Green</button>
</p>
<p>
<button data-id="3" class="btnbtn-danger btn-lgbtn-
block">Red</button>
</p>

<h1 id="location-name"></h1>
<h2 id="weather-main"></h2>
<p id="weather-description"></p>
</div>
<script type="text/javascript" src="cordova.js"></script>
<script type="text/javascript" src="http://localhost:5000/socket.
io/socket.io.js"></script
>
<script type="text/javascript">
var socket = io('http://localhost:5000');

var buttons = document.querySelectorAll('button');

for (vari = 0; i<buttons.length; i++) {
buttons[i].addEventListener('click', function (e) {
```

```
var body = document.querySelector('body'),
index = e.target.getAttribute('data-id'),
backgroundColor;

socket.emit('button-tap', index);

switch (index) {
case '1':
backgroundColor = 'bg-primary';
break;
case '2':
backgroundColor = 'bg-success';
break;
case '3':
backgroundColor = 'bg-danger';
break;
                        }

body.setAttribute('class', backgroundColor);
                    });
                }
</script>
</body>
</html>
```

The output will look like the following screenshot:

6. Now, start your server and open the app by using the `cordova emulate ios` command. The `dashboard.html` file we created is not being served by our Socket.IO server, so we need to either start a server to serve it up from, or open it directly in our filesystem. Once the app and dashboard are both available, try clicking on some buttons on the app. You should see the numbers on the analytics tool increment, as you expected.

How it works...

In this recipe, our server is acting as an intermediary between the mobile app and our analytics tool. When we tap a button on the app, the server is notified, and the data is emitted so that the analytics dashboard can see it.

We are not persisting the data. If you refresh your dashboard page, the counts will all be lost. In a production scenario, we would probably be writing the count data to a database so that we could access it even after a page refresh.

Doing server-side pagination

When you have a large amount of data, it is often beneficial to present it in paged format so that you don't have to load all of it at once. In this recipe, we will create an app with several pages of data that will require server-side pagination.

Getting ready

For this recipe, we will use a library called `Chance` to generate a large set of random data. Chance is composed of various functions that allow us to get all sorts of random data to test with. So, it is ideal to mock up data before you have any. It can be installed by running `npm install chance` in your command line.

How to do it...

To do server-side pagination using Socket.IO, follow these steps:

1. First, we will create our new Cordova app by running `cordova create app com.server.paginationserverPagination`.
2. Next, we will add the iOS platform by running `cordova platform add ios`, and build it by running `cordova build ios`.

3. Now, we will create our `server.js` file. We will generate around hundred random items when the server starts and selectively provide a subset of the data when the client-side app emits a page-change event. We will also emit some information about the pages so that the client can tell how many records are being displayed per page, which page we are currently on, and the total number of pages:

```
var server = require('http').createServer(),
io = require('socket.io')(server),
    Chance = require('chance'),
chance = new Chance(),
cats = [];

// Generate a random cat with chance
functionrandomCat () {
return {
name: chance.name({ prefix: true }),
age: chance.age(),
twitter: chance.twitter(),
email: chance.email(),
website: chance.url(),
image: 'http://lorempixel.com/50/50/cats/' +
chance.integer({min: 1, max: 10})
    };
}

// Generate a bunch of random cats
for (vari = 0; i< 200; i++) {
cats.push(randomCat());
}

io.sockets.on('connection', function (socket) {
socket.on('get-page', function (data) {
varcatsOnPage = [],
startAt = data.page * data.per,
endAt = startAt + data.per;

        // If there are not enough cats to show in one page
if (cats.length<endAt) {
endAt = cats.length;
        }
```

```
for (vari = startAt; i<endAt; i++) {
catsOnPage.push(cats[i]);
        }

io.sockets.emit('render-page', {
cats: catsOnPage,
pages: {
per: data.per,
page: data.page,
last: parseInt(cats.length / data.per, 10)
            }
        });
    });
});

server.listen(5000);
```

4. The `index.html` file inside the app we created will have a few template elements to render our UI into once it comes available:

```
<!DOCTYPE html>
<html>
<head>
<meta charset="utf-8" />
<meta name="format-detection" content="telephone=no" />
<meta name="viewport" content="user-scalable=no, initial-
scale=1, maximum-scale=1, minimum-scale=1, width=device-
width, height=device-height, target-densitydpi=device-dpi"
/>
<meta name="msapplication-tap-highlight" content="no" />
<linkrel="stylesheet"
href="http://bootswatch.com/slate/bootstrap.min.css" />
<title>My Cats</title>
</head>
<body>
<div class="container">
<h1>My Cats</h1>
<nav>
<ul class="pagination"></ul>
</nav>
<div id="cats-list"></div>
</div>
<script type="text/javascript" src="cordova.js"></script>
<script type="text/javascript"
src="http://localhost:5000/socket.io/socket.io.js"></script>
```

```
<script type="text/javascript" src="js/index.js"></script>
</body>
</html>
```

5. Our `js/index.js` file will be responsible for emitting events to the server every time a page change is requested, or on the initial app load. It will also render the pages based on the data that will be emitted from the server:

```
var socket = io('http://localhost:5000'),
list = document.getElementById('cats-list'),
pagination = document.querySelector('.pagination');

functionrenderPage (cats) {
list.innerHTML = '';

cats.forEach(function (cat) {
varcatElement = document.createElement('div');

catElement.setAttribute('class', 'panel panel-default');
catElement.innerHTML =  '<div class="panel-heading">' +
            '<h3 class="panel-title"><imgsrc="' + cat.image
+ '" />  ' + cat.name + '</h3>' +
        '</div>' +
        '<div class="panel-body">' +
            '<p><strong>Age:</strong> ' + cat.age + '</p>'
+
            '<p><strong>Email:</strong> ' + cat.email +
'</p>' +
            '<p><strong>Twitter:</strong> ' + cat.twitter +
'</p>' +
            '<p><strong>Website:</strong> ' + cat.website +
'</p>' +
        '</div>';

list.appendChild(catElement);
    });
}

functiongoToPage (page) {
socket.emit('get-page', {
page: page,
per: 25
    });
}
```

```
functionpageClick (e) {
e.preventDefault();
goToPage(parseInt(e.target.innerHTML, 10));
}

functionrenderPageNumber (i, active) {
var li = document.createElement('li'),
a = document.createElement('a');

if (active) {
li.setAttribute('class', 'active');
    }

a.innerHTML = i;
a.setAttribute('href', '#');
a.addEventListener('click', pageClick);

li.appendChild(a);
pagination.appendChild(li);
}

functionrenderPagination (pages) {
pagination.innerHTML = '', pageElements = [];
for (vari = 1; i<pages.last; i++) {
renderPageNumber(i, i === pages.page);
    }
}

socket.on('render-page', function (data) {
renderPage(data.cats);
renderPagination(data.pages);
});

document.addEventListener('deviceready', function () {
goToPage(1);
});
```

6. Now, we can start our node server and then run `cordova emulate ios` in your terminal to see the app.

How it works...

When our app boots up, it emits an event to the server asking for the data for the first page. The server computes the data that will go on the first page, as well as some metadata to render the page numbers. All the data is emitted back to the original socket. This socket is able to draw the pages and pagination UI based on the information it receives:

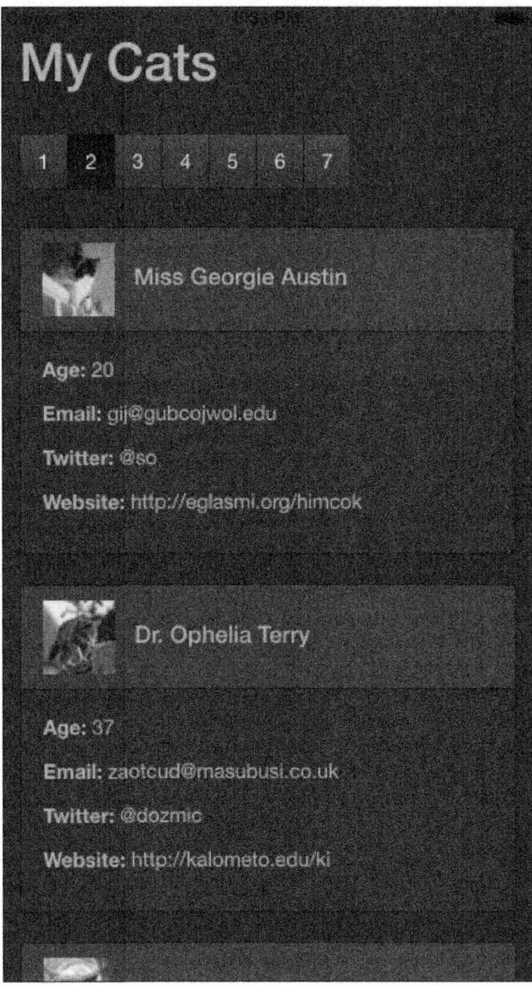

Triggering hot deploys

One of the more frustrating things about developing mobile apps is that when you find a bug or have a new feature to implement, getting your new app into the hands of your users is not as simple as just deploying it, like you would in the web world. Both iOS and Android apps must undergo a review process, which means that you could potentially be waiting up to a week for your update to go live.

Fortunately, if we use JavaScript to write our applications, we will emit changes with Socket.IO whenever our code is updated. We can refresh the app in real time to reflect our new code.

How to do it...

To trigger a hot deploy in Cordova by using Socket.IO, follow these steps:

1. First, we will create our Cordova app by running `cordova create app com.hot.deployHotDeploy`.
2. We will create a `server.js` file that will live outside our Cordova app. This file will be responsible for emitting events whenever the `myFile.js` file changes:

```
var express = require('express'),
app = express(),
http = require('http'),
fs = require('fs'),
path = require('path'), io, server;

app.use(express.static(__dirname));

server = http.Server(app);
server.listen(5000);

io = require('socket.io')(server);

varfilePath = path.resolve(__dirname, './myFile.js');

fs.watchFile(filePath, function () {
io.sockets.emit('code-change');
});
```

3. In our Cordova app, we will point to the `myFile.js` script in our `index.html` file:

```
<h1 id="container">
    Loading
</h1>
<script type="text/javascript" src="cordova.js"></script>
<script type="text/javascript"
src="http://localhost:5000/socket.io/socket.io.js"></script
>
<script type="text/javascript" src="js/index.js"></script>
<script type="text/javascript"
src="http://localhost:5000/myFile.js"></script>
```

4. Finally, our `myFile.js` file will go outside our Cordova app with our server. We will need to start it out as an incremental counter. However, we will be able to save this file again and get new results when it *hot-reloads* the app:

```
app.initialize();

var socket = io('http://localhost:5000');

socket.on('code-change', function () {
window.location = window.location;
});

vari = 0;
setInterval(function () {
    // Change the thing text set in the container to see
the app refresh
    // and display the new code
document.getElementById('container').innerHTML = '#' + i;
i++;
}, 500);
```

5. Now, open your app by running `cordovaemulateios`. You will see a counter that increments over time. If you change the code in `myFile.js`, the app will refresh, and the new code will run instead of the old code:

How it works...

In our application, we saw an initial counter that increments over time. However, we have a file watcher in our node application. This file watcher will trigger a Socket.IO event whenever the file changes. The client side listens for the change event to fire, and reacts by reloading the entire page.

Reloading the entire app is not always ideal. Using technology such as the WebPack package bundler, we could actually be more selective about the code that we refresh, and append code changes a-la-carte, instead of blowing away everything each time the app updates.

Index

T

Thank you for buying
Socket.IO Cookbook

About Packt Publishing

Packt, pronounced 'packed', published its first book, *Mastering phpMyAdmin for Effective MySQL Management*, in April 2004, and subsequently continued to specialize in publishing highly focused books on specific technologies and solutions.

Our books and publications share the experiences of your fellow IT professionals in adapting and customizing today's systems, applications, and frameworks. Our solution-based books give you the knowledge and power to customize the software and technologies you're using to get the job done. Packt books are more specific and less general than the IT books you have seen in the past. Our unique business model allows us to bring you more focused information, giving you more of what you need to know, and less of what you don't.

Packt is a modern yet unique publishing company that focuses on producing quality, cutting-edge books for communities of developers, administrators, and newbies alike. For more information, please visit our website at `www.packtpub.com`.

About Packt Open Source

In 2010, Packt launched two new brands, Packt Open Source and Packt Enterprise, in order to continue its focus on specialization. This book is part of the Packt open source brand, home to books published on software built around open source licenses, and offering information to anybody from advanced developers to budding web designers. The Open Source brand also runs Packt's open source Royalty Scheme, by which Packt gives a royalty to each open source project about whose software a book is sold.

Writing for Packt

We welcome all inquiries from people who are interested in authoring. Book proposals should be sent to `author@packtpub.com`. If your book idea is still at an early stage and you would like to discuss it first before writing a formal book proposal, then please contact us; one of our commissioning editors will get in touch with you.

We're not just looking for published authors; if you have strong technical skills but no writing experience, our experienced editors can help you develop a writing career, or simply get some additional reward for your expertise.

Socket.IO Real-time Web Application Development

ISBN: 978-1-78216-078-6 Paperback: 140 pages

Build modern real-time web applications powered by Socket.IO

1. Understand the usage of various socket.io features like rooms, namespaces, and sessions.
2. Secure the socket.io communication.
3. Deploy and scale your socket.io and Node.js applications in production.
4. A practical guide that quickly gets you up and running with socket.io.

Building Scalable Apps with Redis and Node.js

ISBN: 978-1-78398-448-0 Paperback: 316 pages

Develop customized, scalable web apps through the integration of powerful Node.js frameworks

1. Design a simple application and turn it into the next Instagram.
2. Integrate utilities such as Redis, Socket.io, and Backbone to create Node.js web applications.
3. Learn to develop a complete web application right from the frontend to the backend in a streamlined manner.

Please check **www.PacktPub.com** for information on our titles

Printed in Great Britain
by Amazon